A HOME
FOR EVERY
PLANT

This book is dedicated to Professor Kingsley Dixon
and everyone who cares about our world
and its plants. —MB

To my family, who taught me sensitivity
to my surroundings, and to my vegetable
family, who taught me the rest.
—LP

Phaidon Press Inc.
65 Bleecker Street
New York, NY 10012

phaidon.com

First published 2023
© 2023 Phaidon Press Limited
Text copyright Matthew Biggs © 2023
Illustrations copyright Lucila Perini © 2023

Artwork created digitally

ISBN 978 1 83866 697 2 (US edition)
004-0223

A CIP catalog record for this book is available from the
Library of Congress.

Printed in China

Commissioning Editor: Maya Gartner
Project Editor: Alice-May Bermingham
Production Controller: Rebecca Price
Design: Ana Teodoro, Cantina

Words highlighted in **bold** are described in the glossary at
the back of the book (p124). Words in *italics* are the plants'
Latin name. This is the scientific name they are known as
worldwide. Throughout this book we have mainly referred
to the plants by their common name. Common names are like
a nickname, they can be different around the world.

Written by Matthew Biggs
Illustrations by Lucila Perini

A HOME FOR EVERY PLANT

Wonders of the
Botanical World

Contents

A WORLD FULL OF PLANTS

Plants are all around us, but because they don't move or talk to each other the way that we do, and they don't bark, meow, or roar to attract our attention, it is easy to forget how important they are. In fact, our eyes see green more easily than any other color, so plants just fade into the background. Scientists call this "plant blindness," but don't worry, it can easily be cured!

If we open our eyes and really look, plants are everywhere doing amazing things, such as flowers that smell of cheese to attract mice as **pollinators**, leaves that change shape to hide from predators, and an overlooked bog plant that helps protect our planet. Plants also make the furniture we sit on, the vegetables we eat, and the oxygen we breathe!

This book reveals the hidden secrets of some of world's most extraordinary plants by journeying through some of Earth's coldest, wettest, hottest, and driest places. You will learn how plants survive even in extreme environments, and how important they are to our Earth, and to us! Through learning about their **habitats**, you can discover how to grow and take care of some incredible plants yourself.

Welcome to the world of plants.

What Is a Plant?

Plants are living things that grow on earth, in water, or on other plants. If you have roots instead of toes and feet, and a stem instead of legs and a body . . . if you have branches and twigs instead of arms and fingers, and veins in your leaves but not in your body . . . if you breathe in CO_2 and breathe out oxygen, are green and can turn sunlight into energy, then you are a plant.

Let's take a look at the most important parts of a plant.

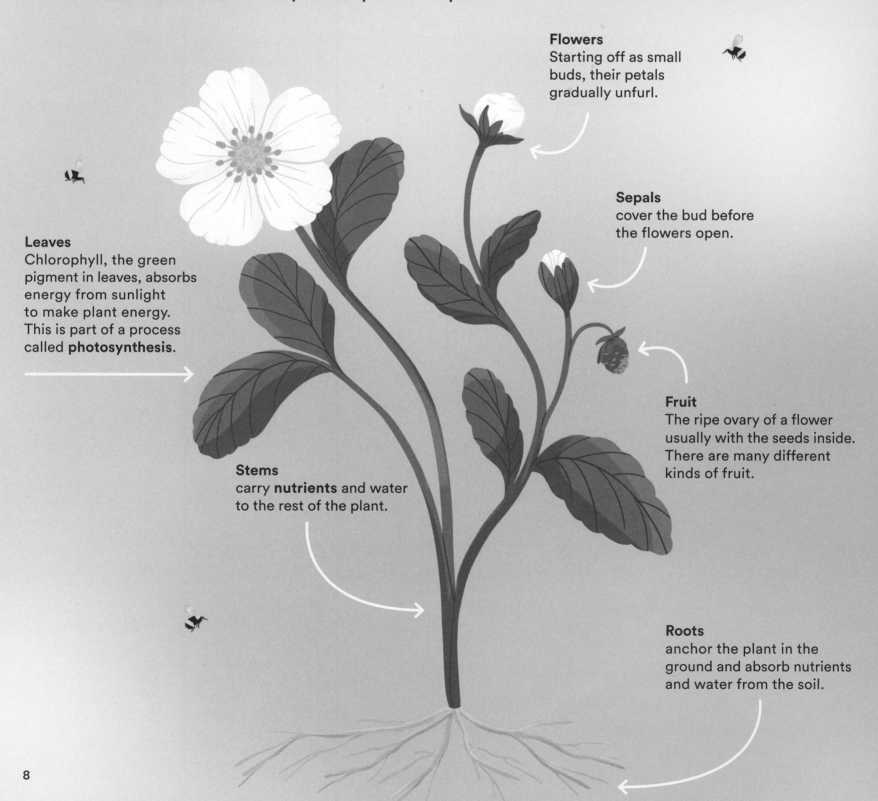

Flowers
Starting off as small buds, their petals gradually unfurl.

Sepals
cover the bud before the flowers open.

Leaves
Chlorophyll, the green pigment in leaves, absorbs energy from sunlight to make plant energy. This is part of a process called **photosynthesis**.

Fruit
The ripe ovary of a flower usually with the seeds inside. There are many different kinds of fruit.

Stems
carry **nutrients** and water to the rest of the plant.

Roots
anchor the plant in the ground and absorb nutrients and water from the soil.

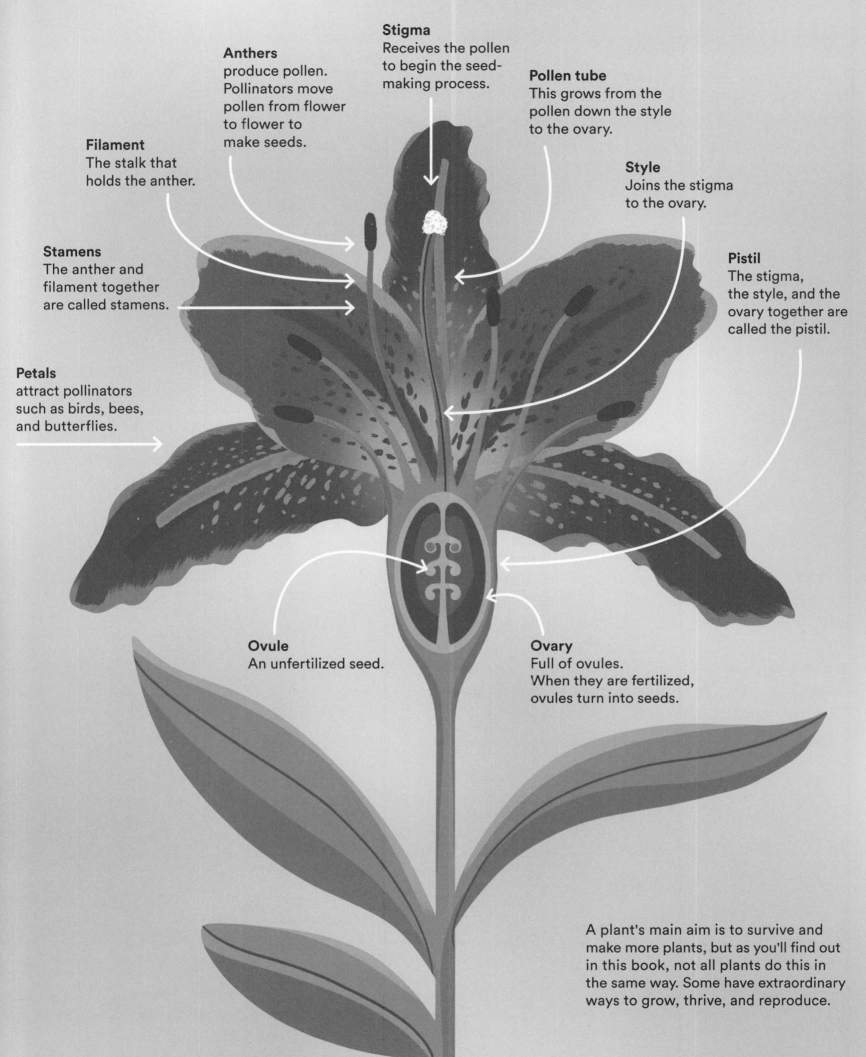

Anthers
produce pollen.
Pollinators move
pollen from flower
to flower to
make seeds.

Stigma
Receives the pollen
to begin the seed-
making process.

Pollen tube
This grows from the
pollen down the style
to the ovary.

Filament
The stalk that
holds the anther.

Style
Joins the stigma
to the ovary.

Stamens
The anther and
filament together
are called stamens.

Pistil
The stigma,
the style, and the
ovary together are
called the pistil.

Petals
attract pollinators
such as birds, bees,
and butterflies.

Ovule
An unfertilized seed.

Ovary
Full of ovules.
When they are fertilized,
ovules turn into seeds.

A plant's main aim is to survive and
make more plants, but as you'll find out
in this book, not all plants do this in
the same way. Some have extraordinary
ways to grow, thrive, and reproduce.

What Is a Habitat?

A habitat is a place where living things make their home. Ideally, a habitat provides everything a living thing needs to thrive, but that is not always possible. Plants need the right combination of light, soil, water, food, temperature, and **humidity** but they can adapt. Different plants have different needs. A desert cactus can't live in the rain forest and a large-leaved rain forest plant can't live in the desert.

On your journey around the world you will visit six different **climates**. The climates you will travel through are adapted from the Köppen classification, invented by botanist Wladimir Köppen (1846–1943), who based his climatic zones on the plants that lived in each area.

Each climate is divided into different habitats. You are about to discover the coolest plants that live in each habitat, from the giant baobab in the grasslands of Africa, whose trunk can be big enough to store 3,000 gallons of water, to the tiniest flowering plant in the world, which can sail through the eye of a needle.

Understanding the habitat is key to being a good plant pal. Copy these conditions and you can grow some of these weird and wonderful plants at home.

Tropic of Cancer

Equator

Tropic of Capricorn

These are the amazing climates . . .

TROPICAL

The tropics run on either side of the equator, between the Tropic of Cancer and the Tropic of Capricorn. It is hot all year-round and can be very humid. Areas bordering the tropics are called "subtropics."

MEDITERRANEAN

Mediterranean climates are found in several places around the world, not just in the Mediterranean. It is hot and dry in summer, and cool and wet in winter.

TEMPERATE

The **weather** changes from day to day, but is rarely extreme. Winters are cool, with some frost and snow. Rainfall is spread throughout the year.

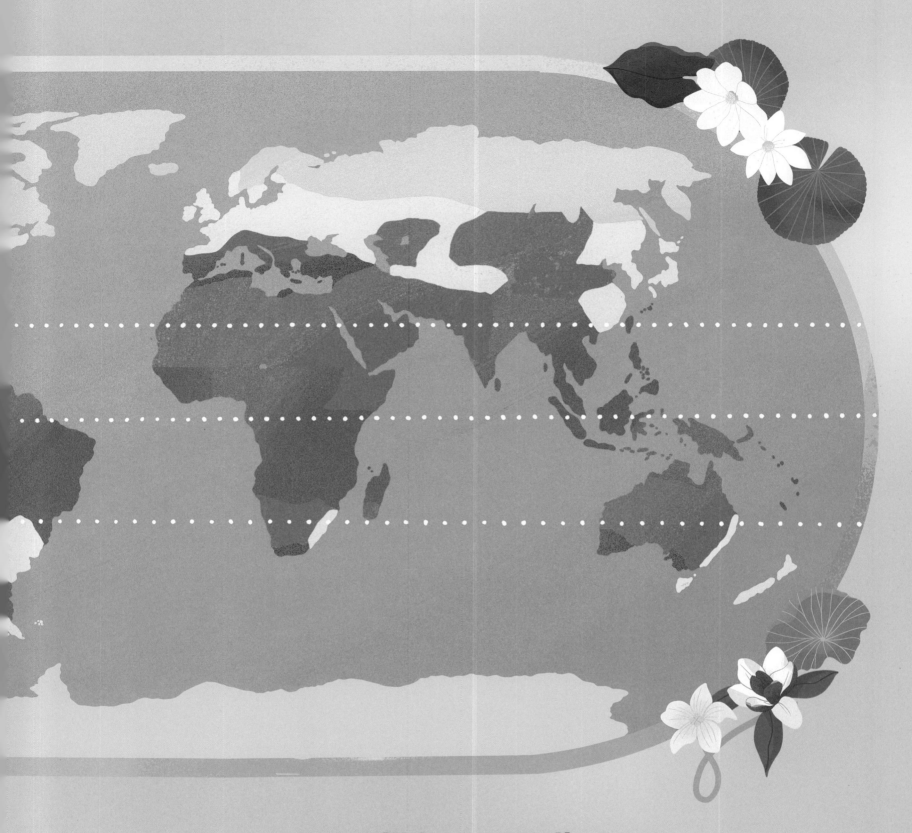

. . . we will be traveling to.

ARID

Arid climates are very dry and most are very hot. Some have seasonal rainfall; in others, droughts can last for years. It can be extremely hot in the day and temperatures plummet at night.

COLD

Near the North and South poles, summers are short and some areas are permanently covered in snow. It can also be very cold at the top of high mountains in otherwise hot areas.

AQUATIC

Lakes, streams, and rivers are found in most different climatic zones, even in deserts after heavy rain, though they soon evaporate. They don't appear in places where the water is permanently frozen.

TROPICAL

Welcome to the tropics, home to most of the world's rain forests and more than half of the world's plants. The tropics "belt" stretches around the middle part of Earth, close to the equator, where sunlight is at its strongest. Rain forests here are often hot and **humid**, with rain, which is vital to plant growth, almost every day. Some tropical areas have wet and dry seasons. In dry seasons, plants on the African savanna store water or go **dormant** to survive. In wet seasons, heavy rains known as monsoons bring up to forty feet of rain—some of the planet's wettest weather—to the foothills of the Himalayan mountain range in Asia. The only place the **weather** gets cooler in the tropics is high up in the mountains. Plants here spend most of their life surrounded by cool, damp clouds.

Indonesian Rain Forest

A rain forest is a tropical woodland with tall, leafy trees and lots of rain. Rain forests have four different layers. On the forest floor there are billions of fallen leaves and branches forming a fast-rotting layer that feeds the plants. Between the forest floor and the canopy there is a dense layer of plants called the understory. It is very hot and humid here, with no wind. The canopy is the roof of the rain forest. It is full of leaves and branches. It is so thick, it can take ten minutes for rain to reach the ground. Very tall trees pop out through the top of the canopy, making up the emergent layer. The world's tallest emergent tree can be found in the Indonesian rain forest; at over 305 feet tall, it is as tall as the Statue of Liberty.

Titan Arum
Amorphophallus titanum

This **endangered** plant only grows in the wild in the rain forests of western Indonesia. It is one of the most famous (and stinkiest!) plants in the world.

The titan arum likes to live alone, so the next nearest plant can be 3 mi away.

The titan arum can take up to 7 years to bloom. Before opening, the flower spike grows up to 4 in per day. It can grow up to 10 ft tall.

spike

When the flower is ready for **pollination**, the center heats up, releasing a terrible stench into the air. Insects are attracted to this stinky perfume from up to 1 mi away!

The flower spike only blooms for 24 to 36 hours. During this time, insects visit the flowers thinking it is rotting meat because that's what it smells like! They drop and pick up pollen as they go from plant to plant.

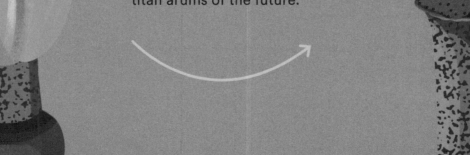

After it is pollinated, the flower collapses— its work is done!

If pollinated, the titan arum plant produces fruit that is eaten by birds such as the rhinoceros hornbill. When the bird poops, seeds from the fruit are scattered through the forest and grow titan arums of the future.

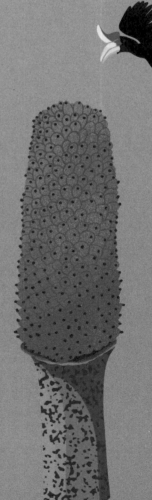

Amazon Rain Forest

The world's largest rain forest is the Amazon in South America. As many as 80,000 plant **species** live here, and plants often find unusual places to thrive. Some rain forest plants steer clear of the crowded understory and forest floor and grow on branches where it is lighter and there are more pollinators. Plants that do this, such as orchids, ferns, and **bromeliads**, are called **epiphytes** and don't need soil to live. They have clever ways of catching and storing water. Some orchids have thick, water-storing stems, while others have "water bottles" at their leaf bases. Zebra urn plants have a waxy coating to help hold water, with a "bucket" in their center to store it.

Zebra Urn Plant
Aechmea zebrina

These bromeliads are very unusual. Their striking striped, almost swordlike leaves provide shelter and food to many small Amazon creatures.

The leaves of zebra urn plants and many other bromeliads are adapted to catch water so it drains into the center. The center of the plant is liquid plant food.

The roots of epiphytes anchor the plant to the tree's branches.

Crabs, flies, beetles, lizards, mosquitos, and small snakes have all been found living in the central part of various species of bromeliads; birds and small animals visit to drink the water.

This is helpful for the bromeliad, which feeds on their poop. Leaves and twigs also fall into the center and rot, providing more **nutrients**. What a lovely diet!

Many tree frogs will spend their whole lives by the bromeliad's "bucket," only climbing down to the ground once a year to breed.

Bromeliads often have brightly colored flowers to attract pollinators.

Some have carnivorous plants living within. Creatures must swim with care!

Mangrove Forests

Mangroves are woody trees or shrubs that grow on the coast in salt water, where most land plants would die. These amazing plants are a bridge between land and sea, taking advantage of all the **sediment** washed down by rivers or moved by the sea. Red mangroves have millions of roots that grow close together. This tangle makes it a safe place for baby crabs, shrimp, and fish to grow, which is why they are called "nursery" **habitats**. Mangrove forest "walls" also protect the coastline against big waves and tropical storms. Mangrove forests cover around 58,688 square miles of Earth's surface. That's twice the size of Scotland!

Mangrove forests are flooded with water every day when the tide comes in. Their masses of roots keep the plant attached to the mud so it isn't washed away.

Mangrove trees and shrubs have different ways to help them survive. Red mangroves prop themselves up with stilt roots. They breathe through bark and filter out salt to get fresh water and air.

Lots of animals make their homes in mangrove forests.

Red Mangrove
Rhizophora mangle

Not many plants like salt water, but red mangrove trees do. They are happy by the seaside and have special features to help them survive.

Black mangroves have breathing roots that stick up above the seawater and wet mud like snorkels. They take up seawater and push the salt out onto the leaves.

The leaves that fall from the trees and sediment that collects around their roots can combine to form islands.

Red mangrove seeds grow roots while still on the tree, then fall in the water and float away. They are ready to grow as soon as they are washed onto the sand.

Savannas

In tropical grasslands, known as savannas, it is warm year-round, though there is a wet and a dry season. Grassland in these regions is dotted with trees and shrubs with tough stems, such as umbrella-shaped acacia trees. Other trees and shrubs, like the baobab, store water to survive the lack of rain. Plants here grow during the rainy season and go dormant as the ground dries out. There are often groups of trees around water holes where animals come to drink. African elephants, zebras, and giraffes that live on the savanna, eating its grasses, shoots, and tree leaves, travel long distances in the dry season to find water here.

Baobab
Adansonia digitata

Baobabs are thought to be the oldest flowering trees alive. They can grow to 98 ft tall and over 32 ft wide and can live for over 1,200 years.

Baobab don't flower until they are at least 15 years old. Each fruit takes about 6 months to ripen. Full of minerals, these fuzzy fruits contain even more vitamin C than an orange.

The baobab's waxy white flowers are the size of saucers. They open at night all at once and only live for 24 hours. They are pollinated by bats, bush babies, and moths.

Hollow inside, the trunk can store about 100 full bathtubs of water. Elephants gouge holes into baobabs to drink the water during a drought; the baobabs heal over time.

Because they are hollow, baobab tree trunks have been used as barns, bus shelters, post offices, prisons, homes, and even a public toilet!

Humans also tap holes to find water.

21

Congo Rain forest

Almost 80 percent of Africa's rain forest is in the Congo Basin, which is the second largest rain forest in the world. About 10,000 species of tropical plants grow there and one-third of them are found nowhere else in the world. The Congo forests are less diverse than other rain forests in the world, but they are still very important "green lungs of the planet." The forest is under threat from deforestation. It is being cleared for farming and mining, and trees are felled for timber. Some of the rarest trees have only been seen once in the last 150 years, so scientists think that they may already be extinct.

Giant Sea Bean
Entada rheedii

This giant plant is a relative of the peas you eat for your dinner. The record-breaking bean pods grow to up to 6.5 ft long. They are the largest bean pods in the world.

The stem of the giant sea bean can grow 1–3 in a day and 32 ft in 6 months. That's the length of a bus!

When they are ripe,
the bean pods turn brown
and fall to the ground.

Each bean pod contains
10 to 15 seeds in single
compartments. Inside each
heart-shaped seed is a
hollow cavity that is full
of air, like a life jacket.

Giant sea bean plants often
grow near rivers, so seeds
may fall into the water. If a
whole pod falls in, it gradually
rots, releasing the seeds.

Seeds that fall into the
Congo Basin's rivers can float
for hundreds of miles before
reaching the sea. They float
in the sea currents up the
coast of Africa, which drift
them as far as Britain and the
Azores in the Atlantic Ocean.
Look out for them when you
next visit the beach.

Meghalaya Rain forest

From June to September, heavy rain pours down across large parts of south Asia. This is called the monsoon season, when up to one foot or rain can fall every day. It turns Meghalaya in northeast India into one of the wettest places in the world. Rivers in the Khasi Hills become torrents, with lush green **vegetation** everywhere you look. Rocks are covered in ferns and moss. Epiphytes cover tree trunks and branches. Shrubs, orchids, bamboos, climbers, and vining plants fill the forests. This special place so full of plants is home to hundreds of different kinds of birds, insects, and animals.

Rubber Plant
Ficus elastica

Sap from the rubber plant was once used to make rubber, but to the people of Meghalaya, the roots are much more important.

Meghalaya has many deep rivers and gorges that cut villages off from one another. It is difficult to travel, especially in the rainy season.

To solve this problem, people from the Khasi and Jaintia communities make bridges from the roots of the rubber plant. They have done this for centuries.

Fast-growing rubber plants are planted near the river. First the trees develop large, wide roots at the base. As they grow older, they sprout lots of thin aerial roots from the branches.

People make bridges by weaving the aerial roots around or through bamboo stems pointed toward the opposite riverbank.

The roots eventually grow together, forming a sturdy bridge.

25

Cloud Forests

This special type of tropical forest is found high in the mountains, right up in the clouds. The **climate** here is cooler than in the rain forest below. Moisture from the clouds gathers on low-growing trees and the rain is heavy, making everything drip with water. Moss loves growing here, especially from the branches of trees, which are filled with orchids, ferns, and bromeliads. Because it is so wet, nutrients that plants would normally find from water or soil are quickly washed away. To survive, some plants here have fascinating ways of finding food.

King Monkey Cup
Nepenthes rajah

Most carnivorous plants trap and then eat insects and animals, but this one prefers eating their poop!

The king monkey cup is only found in the wild on 2 mountains in Borneo.

The king monkey cup has a trap that is the same shape as a toilet!

Mountain tree shrews in the day and summit rats at night visit the king monkey cup to lick nectar from the inside of its lid. The nectar has a chemical that makes them need to poop.

The poop makes excellent plant food. Sometimes unlucky shrews and rats fall into the toilet and the plant eats them, too!

The traps of these plants are among the largest in the world and can hold over 0.5 gallons of liquid, about as much as a large bottle of soda.

Cloud Forest Epiphytes

New Guinea, in the southwestern Pacific Ocean, is the world's largest tropical island. There are over 13,000 different wild plants growing there, more than on any other island in the world. Some plants depend on other plants and wildlife to survive. When we help each other out, we say, "If you scratch my back, I'll scratch yours." In nature this is called symbiosis. Some plants have lots of bird, animal, and insect friends to help them, while others only have one or two. In the cloud forest of Papua New Guinea, the ant plant, an epiphyte that grows on forest trees, has one particular helper.

Ant Plant
Myrmecodia lamii

Ant plants are a strange-looking gang that come in all kinds of shapes and sizes. They get their name from the ants that live inside them, providing the plant with food in return for a place to live.

The swollen stem bases can reach the size of a soccer ball and are protected on the outside by prickles. The surface is covered in holes so the ants can get inside.

Inside are two kinds of rooms connected by hallways.

Those with smooth walls are the nurseries, where the queen ant lays her eggs and baby ants are raised.

Sometimes ants will plant the seeds of the plant they live in nearby to continue growing their colony.

Rooms with rough, warty walls are where the ants leave the leftovers from their meals and their poop. The plant absorbs this and uses it as food.

Growing Tropical Plants at Home

When caring for these plants from tropical climates, remember that their natural habitat is in the hot, steamy jungle.

Peacock Plant
Calathea makoyana

These beautiful plants live in the dark, still, and damp of the forest floor, where they are often soaked in heavy rain. The only bright light they receive is when the sun shines through the trees in the middle of the day. Because light is so scarce, the leaves move to catch the light. At night its leaves fold and bunch together, pointing upward. It's a bit spooky! Grow them in pots inside in bright, indirect sunlight, in a warm spot in damp air, such as a humid bathroom. Let the top of the compost dry out before watering. They will also grow in a shady part of the garden in warmer climates.

Swiss Cheese Plant
Monstera deliciosa

This big and easy-to-grow plant gets its name from its large holes, similar to Swiss cheese from Switzerland. The Swiss cheese plant comes from the tropical rain forests of Central and South America. It **germinates** at ground level, grows across the forest floor, then up tall trees. Copy these conditions at home by growing them in light or shade but not scorching sunshine, in still, humid air, away from chilly drafts. If there is no room for a big tree in your home, grow them up a moss pole or outside in warmer climates. In warmer places, you can see them growing in parks.

Weeping Fig
Ficus benjamina

If you live in the tropics, look out for this tree on streets and in parks and gardens. In cooler climates they are often grown as houseplants. Indoors they like bright light but not scorching sunshine; a little in the morning and afternoon is fine. Place them in a warm humid spot away from dry air and cold drafts. You may have just the right spot in your living room or bedroom. The weeping fig is also known as the strangling fig, as its roots grow tightly around tree trunks. The tree gradually dies from its deadly hug. But don't worry, this plant won't crush your furniture!

Christmas Cactus
Schlumbergera truncata

The Christmas cactus's home is in Brazil, in the Atlantic Forest. There are about 8,000 plants, animals, and insects living there that are found nowhere else on the planet, including a cactus that likes hanging out on tree branches or rock faces in a cool, shady, humid forest. Like its desert cousins, this cactus stores water for when it is dry. Grow them at home in bright light, away from scorching sunshine, in a humid atmosphere or out in the garden in warmer climates. In cooler climates, you can hang them outdoors in the branches of a tree for the summer and they will think they are back in the rain forest. Bring them back indoors in fall.

MEDITERRANEAN

In Mediterranean climates, summers are hot and sunny, and winters are rainy and cooler. This climate is found in an area around the Mediterranean Sea called the Mediterranean Basin, in California, parts of Chile, South Africa, and Australia. **Bulbs** and **perennials** grow in spring or fall when the soil is moist. Their leaves shrivel slowly as the soil dries out. Most trees and shrubs have tough, waxy **evergreen** leaves to save water. Others have gray leaves to reflect sunshine. Many have scented oils to stop them from being eaten. In summer, these oils evaporate in the scorching sunshine and the countryside smells lovely. But as the vegetation dries, fires often start and the dry, oily foliage burns ferociously.

Mediterranean Woodlands

Oak forests—called *montados* in Portugal and *la dehesa* in Spain—have been growing in the Mediterranean for over 9,000 years. Here, cork oak is found in the wild on rocky sunbaked hillsides. When people discovered its bark had hundreds of uses, they planted a good supply. Now, about 60 percent of the world's cork comes from Portugal. In total, the western Mediterranean produces about 330,000 tons of cork each year. Lots of different kinds of plants grow in the forests and many animals, including the Iberian lynx—an endangered "big cat"—live there. About 160 different kinds of birds also call these forests home, including the rare black vulture.

Cork Oak
Quercus suber

The cork oak has thick fire-resistant bark that is full of cracks and crevices. It is the only tree that can regrow its bark after being stripped.

Trees are left to grow for 25 years before they are ready to harvest. They are then harvested by hand every 9 to 12 years. Workers make vertical and horizontal cuts into the bark with a special axe or curved saw, then pull off large pieces. It is a very skilled job.

The oldest and biggest tree that is still harvested is in Portugal. Planted in 1783, it is called the "Whistler Tree" because of all the songbirds that sing in its branches. In 2009 about 1,818 lbs of raw cork was harvested from it. That's enough for 100,000 wine bottle corks!

What can cork be used for?

Cork is a lightweight, natural, and recyclable material that is being used more and more.

Cork contains lots of air, so it can float. Ancient Greeks used cork to keep fishing nets afloat.

The Romans made beehives from cork to keep the bees and honey at a regular temperature.

An average tree makes 4,000 corks.

Cork roofs keep houses cool in summer, and warm in winter.

Cork is used as insulation in space shuttles.

Cork-based car seat upholstery is three times lighter than leather.

35

Chaparral

California's Mediterranean zone is called chaparral. It is made up of evergreen trees and shrubs that can survive hot and dry summers. Many birds and animals live among the plants. As the vegetation is dense and scratchy, cowherds riding their horses through the chaparral wear protective leather leggings called "chaps," named after the region. The vegetation is dry, so it burns easily. Fires in this region used to happen every thirty to 150 years, but now they happen more often, due to increased periods of drought and higher temperatures.

Chaparral Yucca
Hesperoyucca whipplei

One of this region's star plants, it is also known as "our Lord's candle" due to its shape. After flowering, it dies, leaving seeds and a cluster of plantlets at the base to grow in its place.

Chaparral yucca take 5 to 10 years to be fully grown. Then it sends up a flower spike that can grow up to 16 ft tall in only 2 weeks!

The spike produces hundreds of white bell-shaped flowers.

At the base there is a bunch of long stiff leaves up to 3 ft long that end in a sharp point to stop animals from eating them.

The chaparral yucca plant is pollinated by the female California yucca moth, which visits the flowers at night and takes their pollen with her.

She flies to another chaparral yucca plant and lays an egg in a flower, placing pollen deep inside. The flower's seeds also provide food for the growing moth larvae. It creates a special symbiotic relationship between flower and moth.

After the flowers have been pollinated, the plant dies. The stalk dries out and falls apart slowly in the sun.

Fynbos

In South Africa, the Mediterranean zone vegetation is called *fynbos* in Afrikaans, which means "fine bush" in English. Around 9,000 different plants live here, and nearly 6,000 of them are found nowhere else in the world. Many plants of the *fynbos* are small shrubs with hard leaves. There are daisies and orchids, plants that look like reeds called restios, nearly 750 kinds of heaths with brightly colored flowers, and over 1,400 different kinds of plants that grow from bulbs. The most spectacular plants of all are members of the protea family, which have big, bold flowers. Proteas are "fire follower" plants. This means after a fire, the smoke, heat, or burnt soil tells the seeds it is time to germinate.

Sandpaper-Leaf Sugarbush
Protea scabra

This fascinating protea, with rough leaves that give it its name, has an unusual way of pollinating its flowers. It feeds small animals, too.

The sandpaper-leaf sugarbush relies on wildfires on the *fynbos*. The hardy wooden seedpods usually only burst open after fires and are dispersed by the wind.

Its flowers appear in the center of a big tuft of leaves.

Their dull color—yellowy cream ageing to red—tells us they are not trying to attract birds or flying insects.

The flowers are also on the ground so another special pollinator can see them and get to them easily.

In fact, all this, along with the cheesy smell they give off, attracts mice instead! The plant also has lots of nectar that mice like to drink.

They crawl into the flowers to drink the nectar at the flowers' base, picking up pollen on their heads and paws then spreading it far and wide around the *fynbos*.

39

Stony Places

Whenever there is spare ground, a plant usually sees it as a great place to grow. Plants like to fill bare spaces. They grow in cracks in pavements, out of walls, or even at the top of tall buildings and chimneys. So be sure to look out for plants in unusual spots. Many plants in Mediterranean regions make themselves at home on rough stony soil, where the ground is baked hot and dry in summer. To survive, many of them find inventive ways of sending out their seeds.

Squirting Cucumber
Ecballium elaterium

This plant loves hot and rocky places. It has one of the most creative ways of sending out its seeds as far as possible.

This untidy ground-hugging plant creeps over the soil.

It is covered in tough bristly hairs that make it unpleasant for animals to eat.

It produces pale yellow flowers in summer.

Its bulging fruit is filled with a sticky poisonous gel and seeds. When ripe, the capsule explodes, just where the fruit joins the stem.

The seed shoots out at a speed of 33 feet per second, sending the seeds up to 20 feet away—like when a water-filled balloon slips from the end of a tap.

The explosion fires at a perfect angle for a long shot so it can travel as far as possible and not hit any leaves.

This explosion can often happen when triggered by a passing animal. Sometimes the gel-covered seeds stick to the animal's fur, dropping off when the gel dries out.

Kwongan

The name Kwongan comes from an original Aboriginal word for "sand plain." This kind of habitat is found in Southwest Australia, where there is very little rain. Like other Mediterranean habitats, it is a mix of scrubby shrubland and medium-sized trees often growing on poor, sandy soil. Southwest Australia is called a **"Biodiversity Hot Spot"** because there are so many different kinds of plants and animals living there. Kwongan is full of flowers, like the *fynbos* in South Africa. It is home to 70 percent of the over 8,000 kinds of plants native to Southwest Australia, including trees, shrubs, orchids, and bulbs. Many are rare and endangered.

Western Australian Christmas Tree
Nuytsia floribunda

This special tree may look beautiful, but it causes lots of trouble in the Kwongan, especially for other plants.

This tree gets its name from the way it bursts into a cloud of strong-smelling, bright yellow-orange flowers around December.

Like other trees, it has green leaves for **photosynthesis**, but instead of its roots taking up nutrients from the soil, they steal sap from plants up to 360 ft away. That's about the length of a soccer field. It takes just enough food to keep the victim alive so that it has food for life.

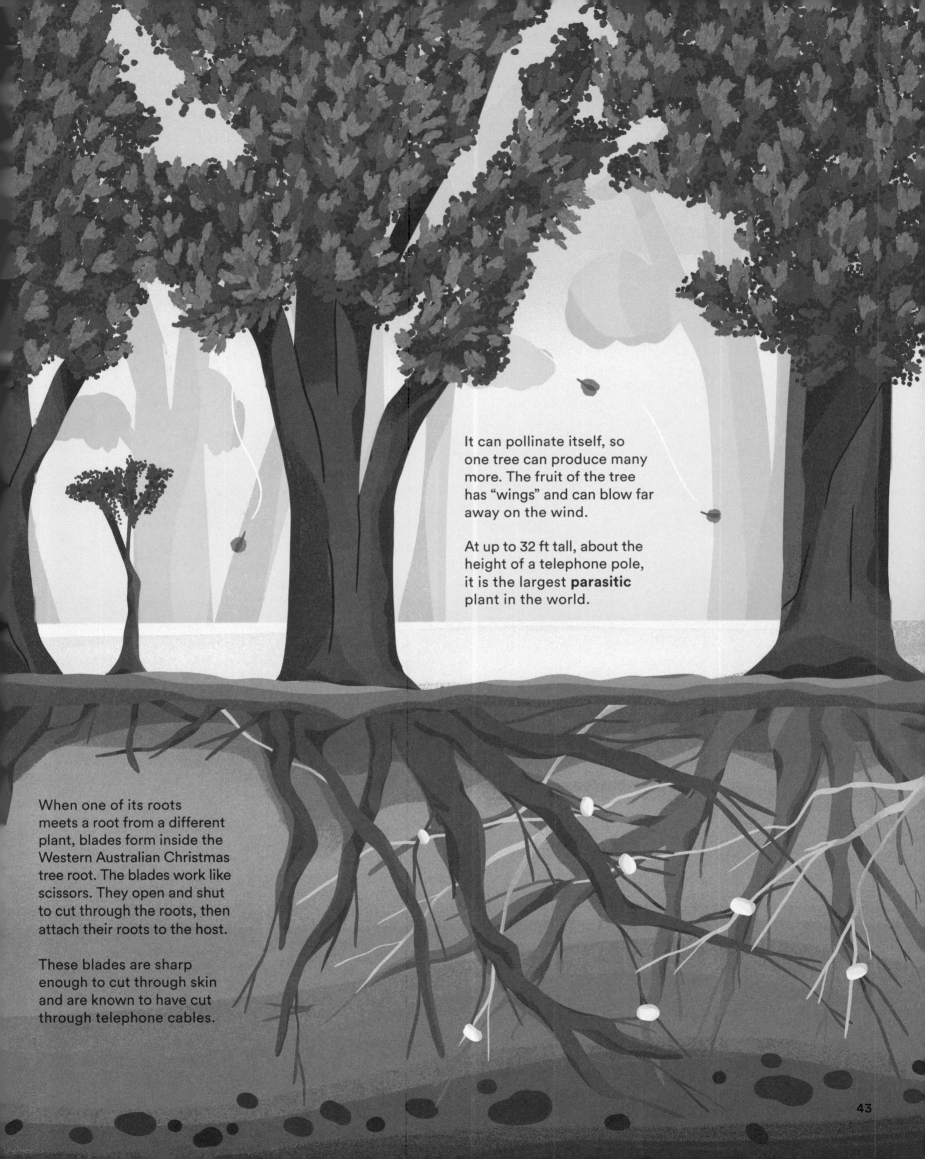

It can pollinate itself, so one tree can produce many more. The fruit of the tree has "wings" and can blow far away on the wind.

At up to 32 ft tall, about the height of a telephone pole, it is the largest **parasitic** plant in the world.

When one of its roots meets a root from a different plant, blades form inside the Western Australian Christmas tree root. The blades work like scissors. They open and shut to cut through the roots, then attach their roots to the host.

These blades are sharp enough to cut through skin and are known to have cut through telephone cables.

Mallee Shrublands

Plants are constantly threatened by humans, who clear land to make space for roads and houses. People even steal rare plants from the wild for their gardens. In the 1890s, people began clearing part of the western Australian bush to grow crops. It became known as the wheat belt. In 1928, an area of eucalyptus and honey myrtle (a type of woody shrub) was burnt and cleared. This brought an amazing plant up to the surface. It was a tiny orchid that flowered underground! No one had ever seen it before. They are still very difficult to find—who knows how many more never-before-seen plants are hiding out there in the "bush"?

Western Underground Orchid
Rhizanthella gardneri

The world is full of incredible plants and there are always some that break the rules, like this one. It is amazing that this orchid even survives!

This orchid remains underground for its whole life with only the flower buds opening at ground level.

Each flower head holds around 150 tightly packed tiny flowers.

Pollen from the flowers is thought to be spread by gnats that crawl down into the flower heads.

Its fleshy fruit then takes 6 months to mature.

It is thought that they live underground because marsupials that used to live underground would then spread its seeds. Scientists think the marsupials would dig up the fragrant seedpods when ripe and disperse the seeds in their poop.

This plant has a clever way to survive in such dry conditions. It uses a special fungus to steal food from the yellow-flowered honey myrtle shrub.

45

Sclerophyll Forest

Sclerophyll means "hard leaf." Plants in this group can survive in a Mediterranean climate where it is hot and dry in summer and the soil is very poor, as their hard leathery leaves are covered in wax, and this helps them save water. In the southern half of Australia, sclerophyll forests are filled with plants such as eucalyptus trees, wattles, and banksias. The forest is alive with fantastic birds and animals, including the eastern gray kangaroo, long-nosed bandicoot, and chocolate wattled bat. It is also home to plenty of parrots and the wonderful fairy-wren. Without plants, these birds and animals would have nowhere to live.

Bitter Bark Tree
Petalostigma pubescens

You will also find the emu here. It helps the bitter bark tree spread its seeds in a very unusual way.

Bitter bark trees bear small yellow-orange fruit divided into 6 to 8 segments, like a tangerine. Inside each segment is a hard stone containing a single seed.

If left on the tree, the fruit dries up and release its seeds.

But emus love the fruit. If one finds a tree, it gobbles up the whole bunch.

Emus eat the fruit whole, digest the flesh, then poop out the seedpods.

They travel over a large area each day, dropping their poop as they go.

There can be over 140 seedpods in one poop.

As the dung and seedpods bake in the hot sunshine, the seedpods dry up and explode.

The seeds end up as far as 8 ft away from the poop.

Now free from the seedpod, each seed has an oil part that attracts ants.

They pick up the seeds, carry them to their nests, and eat the oily part.

The ants put the nibbled seeds outside on their junk pile, where they germinate.

47

Matorral

The matorral in Chile is a mixture of small evergreen trees and shrubs, only ten feet tall at the most, growing close together. It is the only place in South America where this kind of vegetation exists. The soil is rocky and water drains through quickly, so trees often grow in large groups to keep the moisture in. Many of the shrubs and small trees have hard leathery leaves, which make them drought resistant. These plants are called sclerophyllous plants. In the hottest places there are cacti and ground-growing bromeliads. Woodland is also found here, near the coast and at the base of the Andes Mountains.

Soapbark Tree
Quillaja saponaria

This tree may be small, but it can make some incredible things thanks to its bark, which hides a surprising secret.

The soapbark tree is a small evergreen, with dark, glossy leaves and creamy white flowers.

The fruit is an unusual shape. It looks as though the plant has tried balloon modeling!

What can soapbark be used for?

The inner part of the bark contains chemicals called **saponins**, which have multiple uses.

It helps to make foamy toothpaste and beauty products.

It holds together liquids that normally don't mix, such as oil and water.

As soapbark makes things foam and holds moisture, it's sometimes added to foods and beverages.

It has been used by vets to help kill infections in sick fish.

It is an ingredient in several vaccines to help boost the human immune system.

Growing Mediterranean Plants at Home

When caring for plants from Mediterranean climates, remember that their natural habitat has hot, sunny summers with cool rainy winters and they grow on **free-draining soil**.

Lavender
Lavandula angustifolia

Lavender has been popular in gardens for centuries. Bees love visiting the flowers. You hear the buzz, then see the plant. Lavender plants need a sunny spot on free-draining soil and don't like wet roots in winter. In the wild they are grazed by goats. Chop them back about a third into the foliage immediately after flowering. Do this and they last for years. You can save the flowers to make lavender bags.

Common Sage
Salvia officinalis

The leaves from this Mediterranean plant are often used in cooking. It likes hot sunshine in summer and free-draining soil. Don't let the roots get waterlogged in winter. Grow it in a pot of gritty compost or squeeze it into a hanging basket. If you grow it in a pot of gritty compost or a hanging basket, make sure it is watered in summer—it needs a drink from time to time and for that, it depends on you!

Thyme

Thymus vulgaris

This low-growing plant is a bee magnet and makes delicious honey. Crush the leaves and they are fragrant. Most smell of lemon, and some even smell of spicy orange. Some have their own special scents you can't describe—they just smell of thyme! They need free-draining soil and lots of sunshine. Trim them after flowering to keep the plants compact. Or buy a pet goat to do the job for you!

Olive Tree

Olea europaea

Olive trees grow in groves in Mediterranean climates. They need a sheltered sunny position, away from cold winds. Grow them in pots of soil-based compost with added grit. You can also grow them in gardens on free-draining soil, or plant them on a small mound if the ground is a bit wet. Feed them with a balanced liquid fertilizer from spring to fall, when the **weather** is warm and the plant is growing. In cooler climates, protect them from cold weather in winter.

TEMPERATE

Most places in a temperate climate have four
seasons: spring, summer, fall, and winter. Summers
can be warm or hot, winters mild or cold. The weather
changes all the time, sometimes multiple times throughout
the day. Weather changes can be even more sudden
in coastal areas. Most plants have a **growing season**,
which lasts around six months, in spring and summer.
In fall, leaves of **deciduous** trees turn bright colors before
they fall. Plants stop growing in winter when temperatures
drop and daylight levels decrease. Lots of different kinds of
plants grow in temperate climates. There are deciduous
trees and shrubs, grasses, **herbaceous** plants
(plants without woody stems), and **annuals**
(plants that grow for one year and die off).
It is an exciting place to garden.

Deciduous Woodlands

Temperate deciduous woodlands have leafy layers of vegetation. Deciduous trees with large broad leaves will form the canopy. Some light gets through to shade-tolerant shrubs below, with grasses and herbaceous plants forming the ground layer. Bulbs flower in spring then gradually die back as the leaves appear on the trees. Trees, shrubs, and climbers grow new shoots in spring, starting off soft and green and gradually hardening through the summer. By fall the soft young shoots have matured into woody twigs that are tough enough to withstand winter cold. The leaves, too soft to survive cold weather, die and fall.

Sugar Maple
Acer saccharum

The sugar maple, from eastern North America, is famous for its leaf color in the fall. As temperatures drop and the days shorten, green pigment in the leaves breaks down, revealing shades of gold, orange, scarlet, and crimson underneath.

Sugar maples produce sap, a sweet and sugary liquid that contains dissolved nutrients and minerals that help the tree grow.

People tap (make holes in) the trees so sap can drain out. They use sap to make maple syrup. It takes 40 gallons of sap to make about 1 gallon of syrup.

A sapsucker is a kind of woodpecker that makes holes in the bark to sip the sap. Hummingbirds, red squirrels, and wasps also drink sap from the holes.

Sap is collected in February and March. One tree produces from 9 to 15 gallons a season. This makes about 1 quart of syrup.

The sugar maple can be found throughout eastern Canada. Its leaf is the emblem on the Canadian flag.

Its seeds are spread by the wind, spinning around and around like helicopter blades.

Temperate Mountain Forests

There are over 2,500 different kinds of palms in the world. We call them trees because they grow tall, but palms are not like true trees that grow branches and become thicker around the trunk with age. They are in a group of plants called monocots. New leaves grow from a bud at the top of the stem. Palms don't usually branch as they grow. Most palms are found in warm and tropical climates. The Chusan palm is found in the wild in forests that are regrowing after being chopped down and along mountain ridges from the Himalayas all the way down to Vietnam. It is often grown in gardens in cool climates because it survives temperatures down to 30°F and even snow.

Chusan Palm
Trachycarpus fortunei

Wherever the Chusan palm grows, humans and birds have spread its seeds into the wild. In some mountain areas, it has spread into forests, shading out native plants and reducing **biodiversity**.

The leaves, which last for years, are fan-shaped and about 3 ft across.

This palm has been introduced to New Zealand. Its pollen is an important food source for the very rare lesser short-tailed bat.

Each year it usually produces small yellow flowers that dangle down from the leaves in a bunch.

These flowers turn into blue-black fruit, each one about the size of a marble.

Male and female flowers grow on different trees. How can you tell if a plant is male or female? Only female plants produce fruit.

The tall round stem is covered in coarse, dark fibers.

In China, its fibers are used to make ropes, brushes, brooms, and doormats.

They are also used to make clothes, including hats and a rough kind of cape used to protect people's backs when carrying heavy loads, and for rain protection.

57

Wasteland

Not all open, grassy spaces are used by humans; some are left as empty pieces of ground. Plants see these spaces as somewhere to grow. In the countryside they grow on rough shoulders by roadsides or pathways. On farmland, they find space at the ends of fields or between woodlands. In cities they make wasteland by railways, or places where buildings once stood, into their home. And some plants, including weeds, fill the gaps in gardens. Not all plants originate in the countries where they now grow—some plants and seeds, like those found in birdseed, arrive from other countries and find a home.

Greater Burdock
Arctium lappa

This native plant of many temperate zones, including Britain, spreads its seeds in such an incredible way that it inspired a very useful invention.

The greater burdock makes its leaves in one year and flowers the next. Plants that do this are called biennials.

The dark-green leaves grow up to 28 in long and the stems up to 8 ft tall.

Bees love its purple thistle-like flowers that appear in summer.

The seed heads are covered in spines that catch on things.

In 1941, George de Mestral noticed burdock seeds and seed heads stuck to his woolly coat and socks, and to the fur of his dog, Milka. Looking at the seeds under a microscope, George saw the "burrs" had tiny hooks at the ends, to attach to the fur of passing animals. What did this inspire George to invent? Velcro™!

Prairies

The word "prairie" comes from the French word for "meadow." These huge, flat grasslands cover thousands of acres in North America. Temperatures and rainfall are low to moderate, summer is warm and humid, and winters are cold. Prairies were once filled with many different kinds of wildflowers and grasses, but thousands of acres were plowed to grow wheat, so even though much of the soil is rich and fertile, it is one of the most endangered **ecosystems** in the world. Across most of the prairie there is little protection from the strong winds. Some shrubs grow there and a few trees, but most of the plants are herbaceous, and there are different kinds of **perennial** grasses that come back year after year.

Compass Plant
Silphium laciniatum

This sunflower relative is a survivor. One plant produces up to 12 rough-haired stems up to 10 ft tall. In summer it grows yellow flowers well loved by butterflies and birds.

If you are lost on the prairie, the compass plant will show you the way.

You can look at which way the leaves are pointing to tell which direction you are facing.

Although the top leaves are upright, the big lower leaves always point north to south. And if that's not where you are heading, look at the flat leaf surfaces of the more vertical leaves—they face east and west.

New leaves can face any direction. In 2 weeks they twist to point in the right direction.

The flowers are up to 4 in across and grouped near the top of the stem.

Gall wasps find compass plants by tracking the scent of young stems. They lay eggs in the stems, which hatch into larvae. Hundreds can live in each stem.

A long **taproot** grows up to 13 ft into the ground, helping the plant find water during droughts.

Temperate Rain Forests

Unlike tropical rain forests, which are warm and wet, temperate rain forests are cool and wet. They only occur in a few regions around the world, among them parts of the Pacific coast of North America, New Zealand, Tasmania, southwestern Japan, Britain, and the Valdivian forests of southwestern South America. The Valdivian rain forest of Argentina and Chile is one of the few rain forests in the world where there are glaciers. Over half of the plants that grow in this temperate rain forest are found nowhere else in the world. Rocks and branches are draped with mosses of all shapes and sizes. Some trees look like wizards, dressed in cloaks of green. Among them there is a magical plant that scrambles across the forest floor then twines stealthily up into trees.

Boquila
Boquila trifoliolata

Some plants protect themselves with spines. Others have leaves with a horrible taste. This one uses an unusual kind of camouflage to hide from passing pests.

This vine's leaves are usually short and light green with rounded edges.

But when it climbs to another plant or tree, the leaf can change size, shape, color, and even the pattern of its veins to match the leaves of the plant it climbs through.

It is known to have copied over 12 different kinds of plants in the place where it lives.

It mimics the leaves of different plants on the same stem as it crosses from one to the other.

Amazingly, the boquila does not need to touch a plant to match its leaves. Even scientists are not sure how it does this!

By pretending to be the other plant, it hides from anything that is looking for something to eat, especially hungry caterpillars.

Bogs

Bogs often form over ponds and lakes. In cooler climates, they are mostly made up of sphagnum mosses, which form a layer on the surface up to ten feet deep. The old moss beneath eventually dies and rots to form peat. Bogs are an important habitat for wildlife worldwide. Sphagnum mosses keep the area wet and acidic, so only a few other specialized plants, such as cranberry plants, cotton grass, and some carnivorous plants, can grow there. In Canada, moose, beavers, black bears, and the great blue heron find a place to live among the moss. Traditionally, people harvest peat and sphagnum moss. We now know that bogs capture and store vast amounts of carbon from the atmosphere and help to control climate change. This is why Earth-friendly gardeners use peat-free compost instead.

Peat Moss
Sphagnum palustre

Also called the "bog builder." There are over 380 different kinds of sphagnum mosses found throughout the world.

Usually pale green but sometimes dark green, yellow, red, brown, or even pink, the moss floats with a mop-like head held above the water.

Instead of roots and tubes, small holes between the cells allow water to move around inside it.

Much like a giant sponge, sphagnum moss can soak up 20 times its weight in liquid.

It reproduces from spores stored in capsules that keep swelling until they burst like a balloon.

Peat moss captures carbon from the atmosphere and stores it. When it is dug up, it releases this carbon into the atmosphere, so it's better off in the ground!

Its spongelike properties have been used for toilet paper by Vikings and it is a natural antiseptic, so it was used for wound dressings for soldiers in WWI.

Growing Temperate Plants at Home

When caring for plants from temperate zones, remember that in their natural habitat, the weather is rarely extreme. Summers are warm or hot and winters mild or cold.

Wild Daffodil
Narcissus pseudonarcissus

These grow in early spring in temperate climates on streets and in parks and gardens. Plant bulbs in fall pointy end upward in flowerpots of soil-based or peat-free multipurpose compost. Or plant bulbs outdoors in good soil at twice the depth of the bulb, in sunshine or partial shade. In pots make sure they are planted at three to four times the depth of the bulb. Keep the compost or soil moist. Take off the flower heads when they die and let the leaves die back when the flowers have gone. It takes around 6 weeks. They flower year after year when planted in the garden.

Sunflower
Helianthus annuus

Although we think that sunflowers are just tall and bright yellow, there are many different kinds. They like a sheltered position in the garden on fertile soil in hot sunshine. Sow seeds outside 2 in deep in the ground from mid- to late spring. Keep the compost well watered. Cover them with an upturned clear cup to help them germinate quickly. You can also start them off in 3-in flowerpots of peat-free multipurpose compost in early spring. Sow one seed 1 in deep in each pot. When the seedling is big enough to be handled without damage and the root system is nice and strong, plant them outside in the spring when there is no more chance of frost.

English Oak
Quercus robur

In England, scientists are planting "Super Forests" with the correct balance of trees for animals and people, including acorns collected from 1,000-year-old oaks. You can try this too. Collect acorns from under oak trees in fall and plant them in a paper cup with a drainage hole in the bottom using peat-free compost or plant them in your garden. When your tree is about 1 ft tall, dig it up carefully and plant it on the edge of a field or wide-open space. Check on it to see if it is growing happily. It will grow for many years, maybe even 1,000!

Saucer or Chinese Magnolia
Magnolia x soulangeana

There are lots of different kinds of magnolias. You will see them on streets and in parks and gardens. When you plant a magnolia, make sure there is enough space, as it will be much bigger when fully grown. Grow in moist but well-drained neutral to acidic soil in full sun or part shade with shelter from cold winds. Many magnolias flower in spring, before the leaves appear. Plant them away from early-morning sun, as late frosts will damage the buds and flowers.

ARID

Hot deserts are scorching in the day and freezing cold at night, and most of the little rain they receive quickly evaporates in the sun. But even with such extreme conditions, deserts are home to around 1,200 different kinds of plants, all with ingenious survival skills and adaptability! Many people imagine deserts as sandy and dry, but most of them are rocky, and in some there can be rain, fog, or even snow. The hottest air temperature ever recorded on Earth was 135°F at Death Valley in the Mojave Desert in the United States, and the ground temperature can be even hotter. The largest hot desert in the world is the Sahara in northern Africa. Winter temperatures in the Gobi Desert in China and Mongolia fall below -4°F. What plants thrive in these extreme **environments**?

Sonoran Desert

North America's Sonoran Desert can be baking hot in the day and freezing cold at night, with summer and winter rains. Sometimes it even snows. Despite this, it is a desert full of life. Cacti, spiny shrubs, and fast-growing **annuals** all grow here, finding lots of different ways to survive. Most cacti are covered in spiky spines to protect them from hungry and thirsty animals. They also provide shade and collect precious moisture. The surface of cacti are covered in wax, to stop them from losing water. In many, the surface has v-shaped channels so water from dew, fog, and rain runs down to the roots.

Saguaro Cactus
Carnegiea gigantea

This friendly giant is a mass of spines and arms. Lots of animals, insects, and birds make their homes in these cacti, taking great care not to get pricked as they get in.

Because of the dry, rocky soil, most of this cactus's roots sit only just below the ground, but they spread sideways as far as it is tall to gather surface water.

Saguaros can grow up to 40 feet
—that's taller than a telephone
pole—and can weigh up to
12 tons—that's about 2 African
elephants! They can have up
to 25 upward-pointing arms,
which provide food and shelter
for many desert creatures.

The white flowers, which
smell like overripe melons,
are found near the tips of
the stems. Each flower lasts
24 hours, opening at night and
throughout the following day.

The fragrance and nectar
draws bats, bees, and
birds, which help to spread
the cactus's pollen.

Great horned owls and
Harris's hawks nest in
their arms, while gila
woodpeckers make nest
holes in the saguaro's
flesh. Once these birds
finish using the nesting
chamber, other birds, bees,
mammals, or reptiles move
in, meaning the nest can
be used for many years.

After flowering, the bright
red fruit, filled with small
black seeds, packed in juicy
red pulp appears. There can
be 2,000 seeds in one fruit.

Birds and other animals
eat this fruit and disperse
the seeds across the desert
when they poop.

71

Coastal Desert

Some deserts are near the coast. Wind blows in from the sea, but instead of rain, it brings fog, which has smaller water droplets than rain. In the coastal desert of Namibia, the oldest desert in the world, ground temperatures can reach a scorching 149°F. Plants can't rely on the rain, as there is less than half an inch a year, and for many months it doesn't rain at all. Thankfully, every day fog rolls in from the sea. To survive, the welwitschia plant that grows here drinks the fog. This special plant often lives between 300 to 500 years. The longest-living one is even thought to be 2,000 years old! The plant only produces two leaves that last the plant's whole life. That is unusual in the plant world.

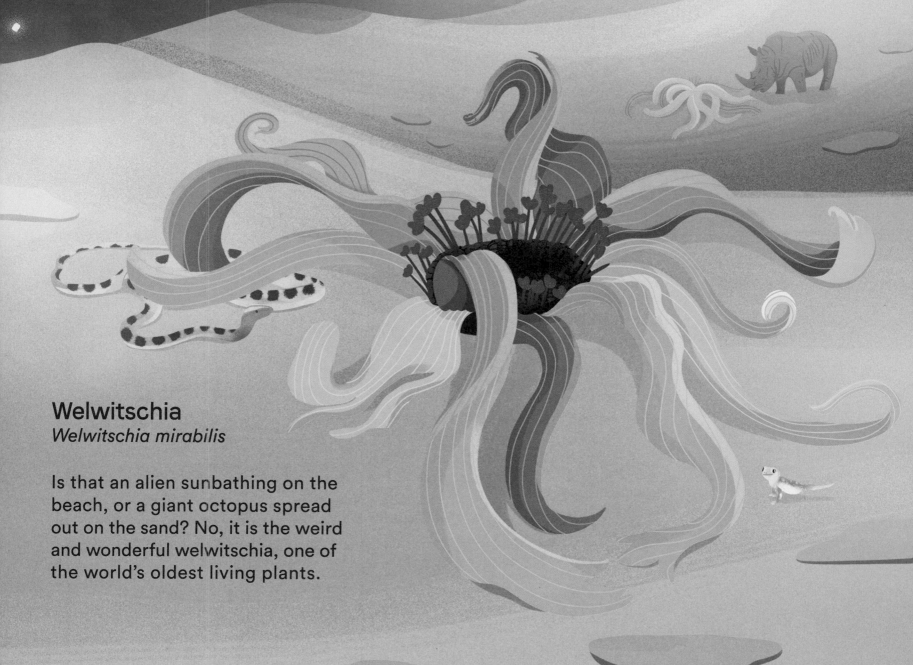

Welwitschia
Welwitschia mirabilis

Is that an alien sunbathing on the beach, or a giant octopus spread out on the sand? No, it is the weird and wonderful welwitschia, one of the world's oldest living plants.

Welwitschia's leaves grow up to 20 ft long. That's longer than a giraffe is tall!

The plant only produces 2 leaves its entire life, but after years of being blown around by strong winds, its 2 leaves are shredded into ribbons, giving the plant its tentacle-like look.

Most desert plants are designed to save water, but the welwitschia doesn't bother. Instead, the leaves have lots of breathing holes. When it is foggy, these breathing holes open. They "breathe" in the fog to get the water they need. They shut the holes when the sun is hot.

The welwitschia is related to pine trees and produces cones, not flowers!

The female cones gradually break down and release the welwitschia's seed. Each white seed has "wings" and is blown away on the wind.

Some fog water runs down channels in the leaves and into the ground. A network of fine roots just below the surface drinks up the water. The welwitschia's huge taproot can reach water up to 10 ft underground.

Welwitschia can make up to 10,000 seeds, but only a few of them germinate. The rest are attacked by fungi or are eaten by desert animals.

Seeds only germinate after heavy rain and can wait a long time before germinating.

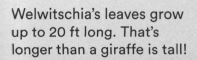

Californian Desert

Some deserts get rain once or twice a year, but some wait for years for the rains to come. In deserts and arid zones of the world, many seeds of annuals stay dormant in the ground during droughts, but when it rains, dust turns to mud and all those seeds spring into action. They grow, bloom, and produce seeds as fast as possible. Once every ten years or so, when there is lots of rain and conditions are just right, deserts such as the Californian desert are taken over by a "superbloom"—one of the fastest and most spectacular wildflower shows on Earth! People travel thousands of miles to admire the beauty of deserts in bloom. There are millions of flowers of all colors. Each one shouts to the pollinators, "Pick me! Pick me!"

California Poppy
Eschscholzia californica

A superbloom turns the desert into a carpet of poppies so brightly colored that satellites in space have even caught them on camera!

The flowering desert attracts insects, birds, and lizards. They come to drink the nectar, lay their eggs, and find food for their offspring.

The birds and lizards also eat those visiting insects.

Even when there is heavy rain, not all of the seeds germinate.

Billions of seeds remain dormant in the ground until the next rains arrive. It can take several years.

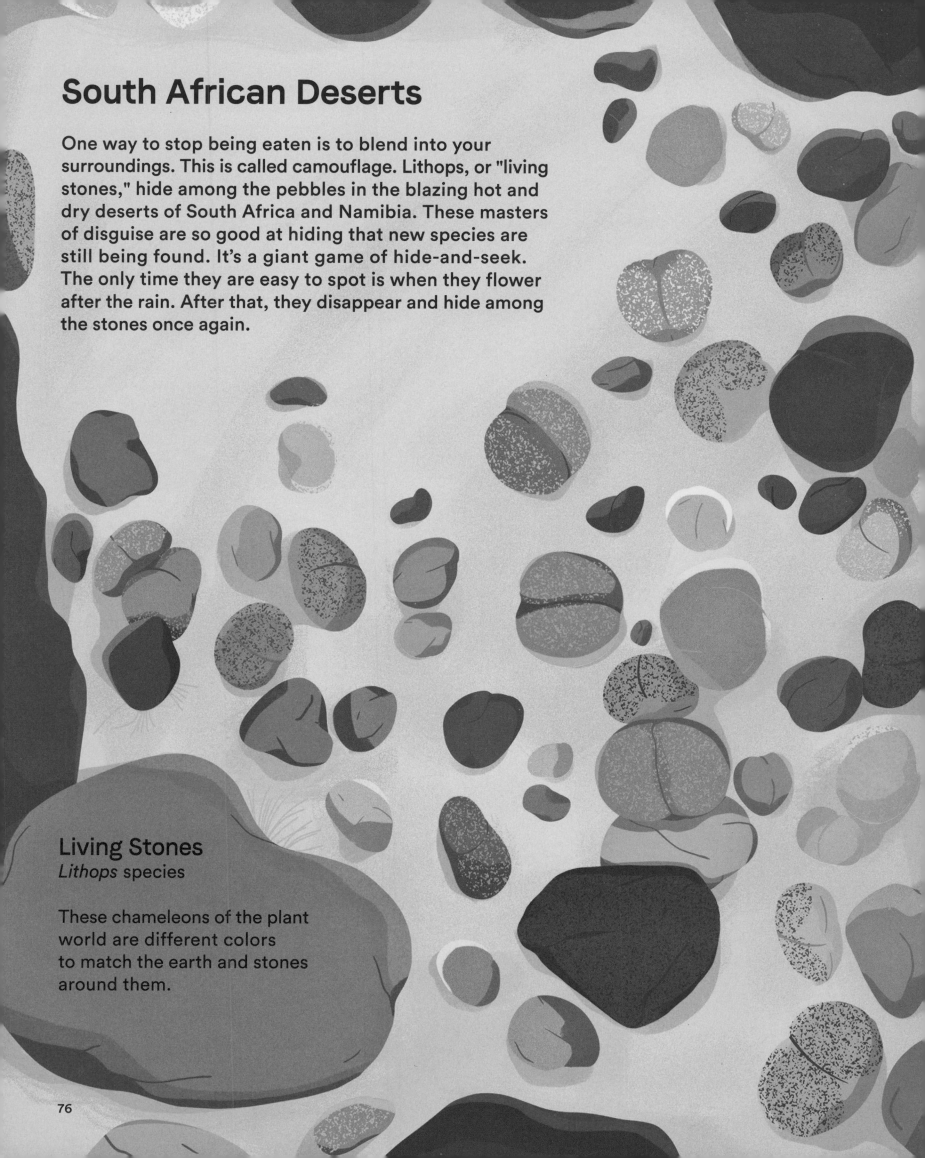

South African Deserts

One way to stop being eaten is to blend into your surroundings. This is called camouflage. Lithops, or "living stones," hide among the pebbles in the blazing hot and dry deserts of South Africa and Namibia. These masters of disguise are so good at hiding that new species are still being found. It's a giant game of hide-and-seek. The only time they are easy to spot is when they flower after the rain. After that, they disappear and hide among the stones once again.

Living Stones
Lithops species

These chameleons of the plant world are different colors to match the earth and stones around them.

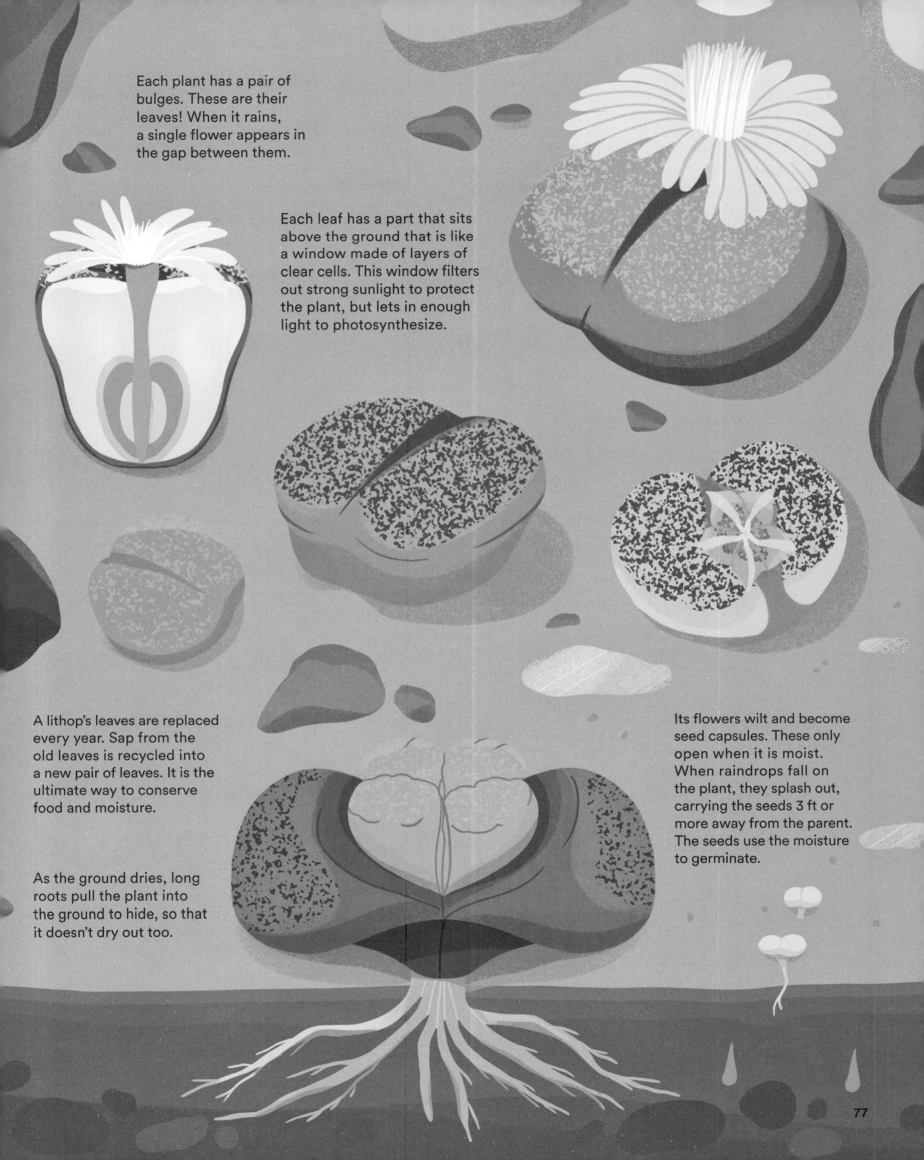

Each plant has a pair of bulges. These are their leaves! When it rains, a single flower appears in the gap between them.

Each leaf has a part that sits above the ground that is like a window made of layers of clear cells. This window filters out strong sunlight to protect the plant, but lets in enough light to photosynthesize.

A lithop's leaves are replaced every year. Sap from the old leaves is recycled into a new pair of leaves. It is the ultimate way to conserve food and moisture.

As the ground dries, long roots pull the plant into the ground to hide, so that it doesn't dry out too.

Its flowers wilt and become seed capsules. These only open when it is moist. When raindrops fall on the plant, they splash out, carrying the seeds 3 ft or more away from the parent. The seeds use the moisture to germinate.

Mojave and Colorado Deserts

The plant world is full of surprises. Most ferns like damp shady places, so what are they doing in the desert? The viscid lip fern is found tucked under boulders on cliffs and rocky slopes and in deserts from California to northwest Mexico. Like lots of other plants, this fern has found a way of surviving intense heat and lack of water. Some have waxy or hairy leaves, while others become shriveled and brown. When it rains, they turn green and spring back to life. Others have small gray leaves or even curl up—all to avoid the sun and keep moisture in!

Viscid Lip Fern
Myriopteris viscida

This fern's leaves produce sticky **resin**, which is how this plant got its name. Viscid means "sticky"! Scientists think that this protects them from being eaten by insects.

These ferns look dead, but when it rains, they will drink up the water and quickly turn green again.

Viscid lip ferns grow under boulders, as it is shady, and when it rains, the water runs off the rock onto the fern. The soil very close to boulders where it is shady also stays damp for longer.

Some desert ferns can lose over 90 percent of their water and still stay alive. The leaves are small, as small leaves lose less water.

The plants' resin makes grains of sand stick to the leaf surface. Scientists think the particles of sand reflect the sunlight so that the leaf does not overheat or scorch in the sunlight.

Occasional rainfall dissolves the sticky resin and washes off the sand so the fern can use its leaves in full to get the light it needs to make energy and grow.

Semi-desert

Around the edges of deserts rainfall is higher than in the desert, so the **environment** changes gradually into a semi-desert. The Great Karoo semi-desert in South Africa is bigger than the whole of Germany and is covered in grasses, shrubs, and small trees. It is home to the bizarre starfish flower, which looks and acts like a cactus but is from a different family. Like cacti, it uses water stored in its stems to make buds and flowers, but stand far back, as this starfish stinks!

Starfish Flower
Stapelia grandiflora

In the Indonesian rain forest, the titan arum attracts pollinators with its bad smell. This stapelia in the desert goes even further —its flowers look rotten too.

As well as looking and smelling like rotten meat, it is also covered in "hairs" to look like the mold on a dead animal.

These "tricks" help to attract flies, which then spread its pollen to other plants, just like bees or butterflies might.

Flies visit the starfish flower, thinking they are about to tuck into a nice lunch, but instead they get a mouthful of pollen that sticks their mouth together.

But before they leave, they do leave behind some eggs. These eventually hatch and turn into maggots, making the flower look even more like . . . dead meat!

The flies spread pollen for the flower, but they've been tricked—they haven't laid their eggs on rotting meat at all.

Seedpods grow in the center of the flower. When ripe, they burst open and their seeds float away on what look like mini parachutes.

Soon there will be stinky starfish in lots of other places.

Growing Arid-Climate Plants at Home

Arid-climate plants like it hot and dry with plenty of bright light and sunshine. They can cope with cool conditions if the compost is kept dry.

Resurrection Plant
Selaginella lepidophylla

This plant originates from the Chihuahuan Desert, which spreads across the United States and Mexico. Summer is hot, but it gets cool in winter and at night. It is one of the easiest plants to grow at home. All you need is a shallow plate of warm water, placed in the sunshine. Put the plant in the water and it unfurls and turns green. Take it out and it gradually dries up and curls back into a ball. It can lose up to 95 percent of its water and still regrow, and can survive with no water for a decade. But it loses the ability to do this if you dry it out too many times!

Golden Barrel Cactus
Echinocactus grusonii

Originally from Mexico, these are eye-catching as indoor plants or in gardens with hotter climates. Grow them indoors in a sunny spot, in special cactus and succulent compost. Water when the compost feels dry in spring and summer. Don't let the compost stay wet, or become too dry. Keep them cool in fall and winter. Water them just enough to stop them from shriveling. Rotate the pot one-quarter of a turn every few days so the whole plant enjoys the sunshine. Feed with cactus and succulent fertilizer in the **growing season**.

String of Hearts
Ceropegia linearis subsp. woodii

This pretty plant comes from South Africa and trails over rocks in the desert sun. It is ideal for indoor hanging baskets or outside in warmer climates. It grows in bright light away from scorching sunshine. Water when the gritty compost is ⅔ dry in spring and summer and when it has almost dried out in winter. (Stick your finger into the compost. Pull it out. If compost sticks to your finger, there is no need to water.) It doesn't mind dry air, but don't put it too close to a radiator. Feed with cactus and succulent fertilizer in the growing season.

Snake Plant
Dracaena trifasciata

This is one of the toughest houseplants, as it will grow in drought, shade, and even in dry air in a drafty room. This arid plant grows happily outdoors in Mediterranean or tropical climates, where it is warm. It likes bright light best. Grow it in cactus and succulent compost. When the compost is dry in the warmer growing season, give it some water. It doesn't need much water in winter. Feed it with cactus and succulent plant food when it is growing. Don't let it get too cold. If you take care of your plant, it produces flowers.

COLD

Cold regions are found in the far north and south of the globe. They are also at the top of very high mountains, even in the tropics. Ice-covered polar regions and mountaintops sit on beds of rock; only mosses and lichen grow there, where there isn't a covering of ice. Away from the permanent ice and snow are the arctic and alpine tundra, which are barren windy places without trees. Ground temperatures here stay below freezing for most of the year—it is called permafrost. In summer the snow disappears and ice in the top few inches of soil melts enough for a variety of plants to grow. The growing season is very short.

High Mountain Screes

High up in the Himalayas the weather can be freezing. It can also be very wet as it is affected by monsoons that hit for a few months every year. The sikkim rhubarb, a cousin of the garden rhubarb, grows on screes near the highest mountains in the world. A scree is a slope covered with loose rocks. They also grow among low-growing shrubs and colourful herbaceous plants that cover the ground. This alpine treasure stands tall in the gaps among them—no wonder these giant plants are easy to see from a distance.

Sikkim Rhubarb
Rheum nobile

These plants show up like bright yellow-green exclamation points, especially against rocky ground. Sikkim rhubarb can be up to 6.5 ft tall and has a root up to 6.5 ft long.

Outside, it can be freezing, but thin, translucent leaves called bracts act like greenhouse windows, keeping the flowers warm.

The bracts filter out the UV light that is very strong in high mountain areas. This stops the sun from damaging the pollen inside and helps the flowers grow faster.

They also shelter the flowers from heavy rain.

Scientists have found that one type of gnat has a symbiotic relationship with the sikkum rhubarb. Visiting gnats collect and spread the plant's pollen when they lay their eggs in the flowers. In return the plant gives the gnat's hatched eggs their first meal!

The long root anchors the plant in place and searches for water, which drains quickly through the stony soil. It also stops it from blowing over.

When the fruit is grown, the bracts open then shrivel up, exposing the fruit so it can be dispersed.

Tundra

These treeless regions are found in the Arctic and on the tops of mountains, where the climate is cold and windy, rainfall is low, and the soil is stony. Only low-growing grasses, **sedges**, shrubs, and alpine perennials grow here. For much of the year, any water is ice and the land is covered with snow, but warmer weather in spring melts the snow and brings bursts of wildflowers such as the narrow-leafed campion. This delicate-looking plant grows in Siberia in Russia, on the tundra and cliffs by the sea, and on mountains in northeast Japan. So how does it survive in these conditions?

Narrow-Leafed Campion
Silene stenophylla

This fragile-looking Arctic wildflower is surprisingly strong. It dies back to ground level during winter to avoid the cold, and its roots stay dormant underground. When the snow melts, it wakes up and starts growing again.

In 2012, scientists found parts of the narrow-leafed campion fruit frozen in the burrows of Ice Age squirrels in Siberia. They had been stored there, perfectly preserved, for around 32,000 years!

They managed to grow these Ice Age plants using cells from the ovary and growing new plants from them. This is called **micropropagation**.

Who would have thought that new plants could grow from prehistoric seeds?

Scientists grew 36 ancient plants. They looked exactly the same as present-day plants until they flowered, when they all produced white flowers with narrower and more spread-out petals.

Amazingly, the Ice Age campions grew for a year, flowered, then produced seeds of their own!

With their starry flowers measuring only ¾ in across and fragile stems, these flowers look too fragile to survive in such a harsh climate.

Ice Age

present-day

89

The Antarctic

Antarctica is what's known as a polar desert, as only small amounts of snow fall each year. It is the biggest desert in the world, twice the size of the Sahara, but rather than sand or rocks, it is almost entirely covered in a massive sheet of ice. To add to this, for six months of the year, the sun doesn't rise above the horizon, leaving the region in almost total darkness. For the rest of the year, the sun doesn't set! Antarctica and its surrounding islands have a harsh climate with a small variety of mosses, liverworts, fungi, and lichens but only two flowering plants: Antarctic hair grass, with clumps that grow in rock crevices on the coast or where the ice has melted; and Antarctic pearlwort, a truly unique survivor.

Antarctic Pearlwort
Colobanthus quitensis

Growing at the end of the world is very hard. It's not warm and cozy like a rain forest, but the Antarctic pearlwort doesn't mind at all. It knows just what to do to survive.

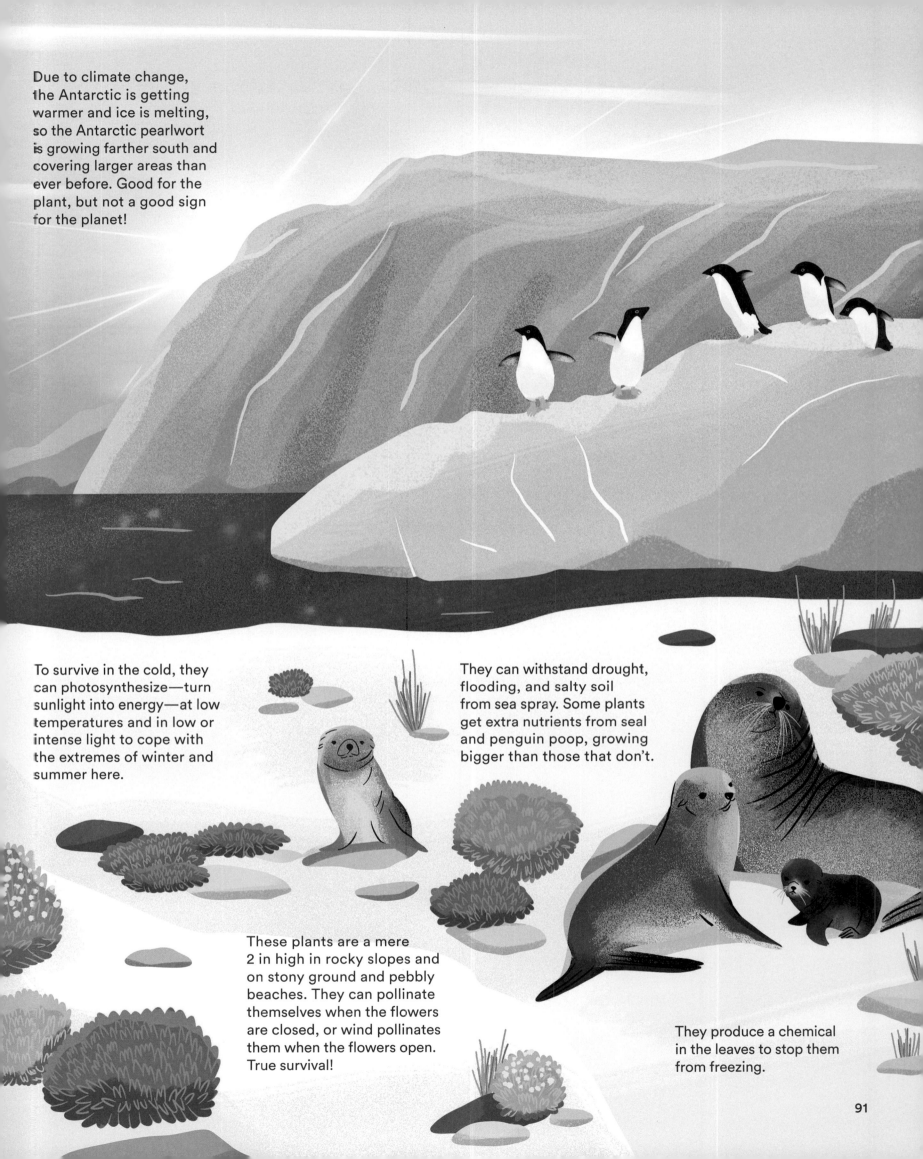

Due to climate change, the Antarctic is getting warmer and ice is melting, so the Antarctic pearlwort is growing farther south and covering larger areas than ever before. Good for the plant, but not a good sign for the planet!

To survive in the cold, they can photosynthesize—turn sunlight into energy—at low temperatures and in low or intense light to cope with the extremes of winter and summer here.

These plants are a mere 2 in high in rocky slopes and on stony ground and pebbly beaches. They can pollinate themselves when the flowers are closed, or wind pollinates them when the flowers open. True survival!

They can withstand drought, flooding, and salty soil from sea spray. Some plants get extra nutrients from seal and penguin poop, growing bigger than those that don't.

They produce a chemical in the leaves to stop them from freezing.

Alpine Grasslands

Lots of different grasses and plants grow in alpine grasslands throughout the world. Winters are long and cold and summers are short. One of the largest areas of alpine grasslands is the Tibetan Plateau in the mountains of Asia. The Puna grassland in South America sits about two to three miles above sea level. It is home to llamas and alpacas as well as the world's biggest bromeliad. This monster relative of the pineapple, known as the Queen of the Andes, is also found in rocky places like cliffs and mountain peaks. It can take thirty to 150 years for it to build up the strength to produce a single flowering spike. Bad weather, a lack of places for the seed to grow, and overgrazing by animals means not many reach adulthood and it has become an endangered species.

Queen of the Andes
Puya raimondii

This record breaker of the plant world is big in every way. It is so tall, it can be seen by satellites in space! It grows high in the mountains, where most plants are very small.

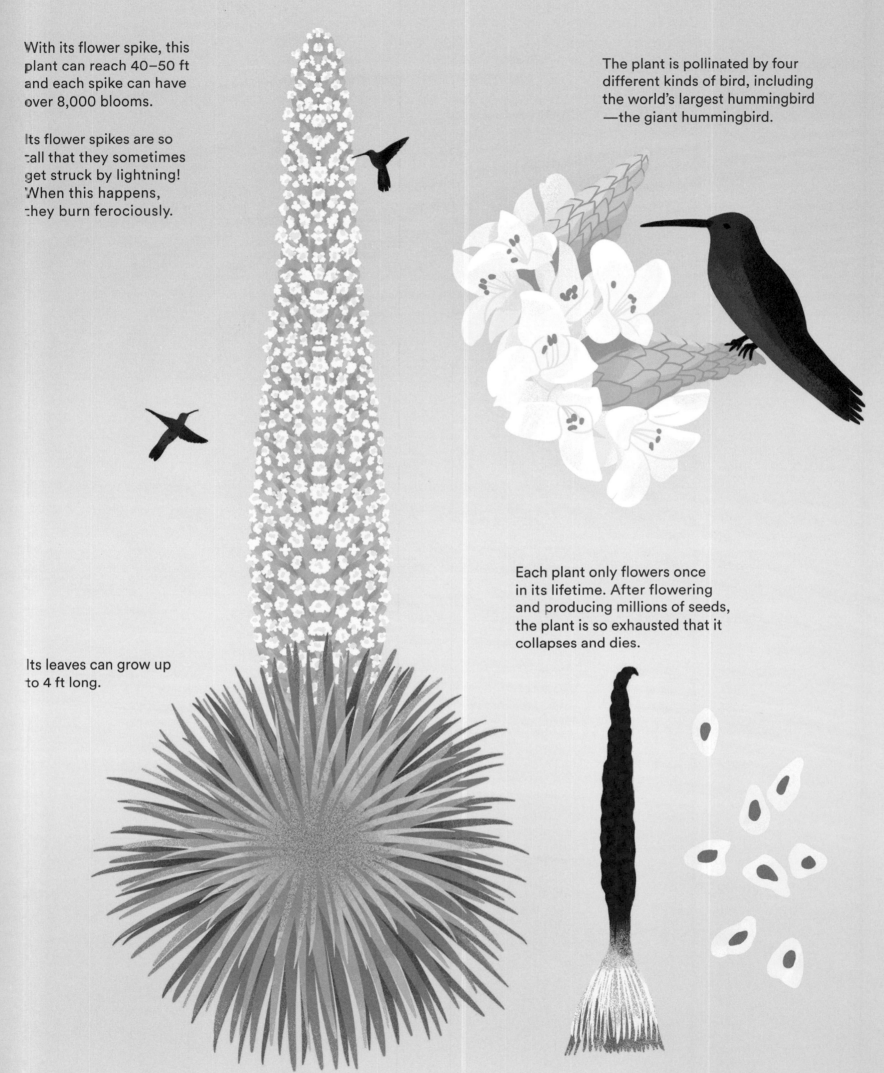

With its flower spike, this plant can reach 40–50 ft and each spike can have over 8,000 blooms.

Its flower spikes are so tall that they sometimes get struck by lightning! When this happens, they burn ferociously.

The plant is pollinated by four different kinds of bird, including the world's largest hummingbird —the giant hummingbird.

Each plant only flowers once in its lifetime. After flowering and producing millions of seeds, the plant is so exhausted that it collapses and dies.

Its leaves can grow up to 4 ft long.

Alpine Meadows

These mountain meadows can be stony with short grass and a few different kinds of plants, or lush green grass and many varieties of flowers. It depends on how high up they are in the mountains, spring and summer temperatures, the kind of soil they grow on, and the amount of available water. Plants will grow in more than one habitat. Cushion plants are found on screes and in stony and grassy alpine meadows. They hunker down against rocks or ground to form smooth mounds in order to survive harsh winters, where they are buried under the snow for several months. You will find plants that are the same shape in deserts, where they also have to survive strong winds, extreme temperatures, drought, and intense sunshine.

Hummock Sandwort
Arenaria polytrichoides

This Himalayan plant may look like a simple cushion lying on the ground, but it has a great many surprising things happening in and around it.

In alpine meadows, water from melting snow and rain drains quickly through the rocky ground. To suck up this water, the cushion plant's roots reach 3 ft down into the ground.

Its mound shape, with its stems tightly packed inside, allows harsh and cold wind to flow over it.

Cushion plants create their own small worlds. Inside their "micro-space," it is warm, moist, and there is plenty of food.

The leaves are tiny and tightly packed so they lose as little water as possible when they breathe.

Only the outer leaves are alive—those inside the mound rot down, and their nutrients are recycled.

In the spring, when the snow melts, they produce lots of tiny white flowers. The plants are often so small that if a rock rolls over them, they are not crushed.

These plants also grow on screes. They can even move with the scree and if the roots are broken, they will quickly regrow.

Mount Everest

There's not much to hold on to when you live on the tallest mountain in the world! Mountainside plants grow on loose rock or crevices in cliff faces. Plants here grow very slowly and live a long time. Mountaineers often collect plants on expeditions up Mount Everest, which, at 29,032 feet tall, is the highest mountain in the world. The highest plants found in the world are the cudweed saw-wort and a cabbage-like plant called the Everest brassica, collected on a rocky scree by Eric Shipton in 1935 at an impressive 20,997 feet above sea level. A few years later Albert Zimmermann found a saxifrage growing in cracks on cliffs at 20,833 feet.

Cudweed Saw-Wort
Saussurea gnaphalodes

It's not just animals that grow wool to keep them warm— some plants do this as well. It also protects them from rain. What a clever thing to do!

The leaves and flowers of the cudweed saw-wort are covered in thick woolly hairs.

These create a **microclimate** protecting the leaf surface from damaging UV light.

The cudweed saw-wort produces new leaves, stems, and flowers every year, then dies back to ground level.

The wool also traps air, stopping the plant from losing too much water in strong winds.

The air trapped in the layer of hairs stays still and warm, so it never gets too hot or too cold.

This plant puts almost all its energy into a good root system. The roots branch at ground level so they can take up nutrients to produce as many leaves and flowers as possible but still stay small.

97

Boreal Forests

Boreal forests form a band around the northern hemisphere of the Earth near the Arctic ice cap. Most of the trees growing in boreal forests, also known as the taiga, are evergreen trees called conifers. They have needles and cones rather than leaves and flowers, and they don't lose their leaves in winter. At the northern edge of the forest, temperatures rarely rise above 50°F in summer, and most of the water the trees drink comes from melting winter snow. The **growing season** is short. In winter it can be very cold and life is tough. Trees here don't grow very tall and the branching is less dense. At the southern edge of the forest, where it is warmer, trees are taller with denser branching, and there are deciduous trees growing among them.

White Spruce
Picea glauca

This grows farther north than any other evergreen tree, nearly to the Arctic Ocean. Here the snow gets very deep in winter. The seeds are dispersed by the wind.

Conifers like these are cone-shaped, with bendy branches. The branches and branchlets are designed to bend so the snow slips off and stops them from breaking.

The needles of conifers growing here have a thick waxy coating to help retain water and protect plant cells from cold winds. Because they are a dark color, they are good at absorbing heat from the sun.

This spruce's broken needles are said to smell of cat pee!

Seeds grow in tough cones, which provide protection during the harsh winter.

As soon as the snow melts and the sun shines, the needles can start photosynthesizing—turning sunlight into energy.

Coniferous trees growing here have thick bark to protect them from the cold.

Growing Cold-Climate Plants at Home

When caring for plants from cold climates, remember that their natural habitat is in cold places often with long, dark winters and long summer days.

Arctic Poppy
Papaver radicatum

This pretty little poppy is found in the Arctic tundra on stony ground. It forms a low cushion of leaves, the flowers fluttering above them like dainty yellow flags. Give it gritty or stony soil in a spot in full sunshine. Or grow it in a soil-based compost with added grit in stone troughs or basins. Take off the dead flowers so more will follow. Cut away the dead leaves at the end of winter and they will regrow in spring, just as they do in the Arctic.

Showy Chinese Gentian
Gentiana sino-ornata

Plant hunters have traveled all over the world searching for the plants to fill our gardens. A Scotsman named George Forrest (1873–1932) visited China seven times for this purpose, working with local people to find plants. He found the beautiful blue showy Chinese gentian in alpine grasslands. You don't need lots of space for alpines. This one is easy to grow and produces lots of flowers. It needs a deep pot or tray with good deep, acidic soil and plenty of rainwater. Keep it in sun or a little shade.

Mountain Avens
Dryas octopetala

The mountain avens is the national flower of Iceland. It is a miniature shrub that is easy to grow. It likes free-draining gritty soil in sunshine but can also grow in part shade. The leaves are like tiny oak leaves and the underside of the leaf is white. It grows close to the ground to hide from the wind. It would be happy at the edge of a garden in a flower border, especially in chalky soil. It flowers in late spring and early summer and with its pretty flowers it could be the star of your garden.

Purple Mountain Saxifrage
Saxifraga oppositifolia

From the mountains and tundra in North America, across the Arctic, and down into Britain and the European Alps, this small but tough plant is found in cold places in the northern part of our planet. It grows at the highest altitude of any flowering plant in Europe. It is happy in a cool, damp climate. It likes sunshine but needs some shade in hot, dry places and should be planted in well-drained cool, damp soil. Pink-purple flowers cover the plant in spring.

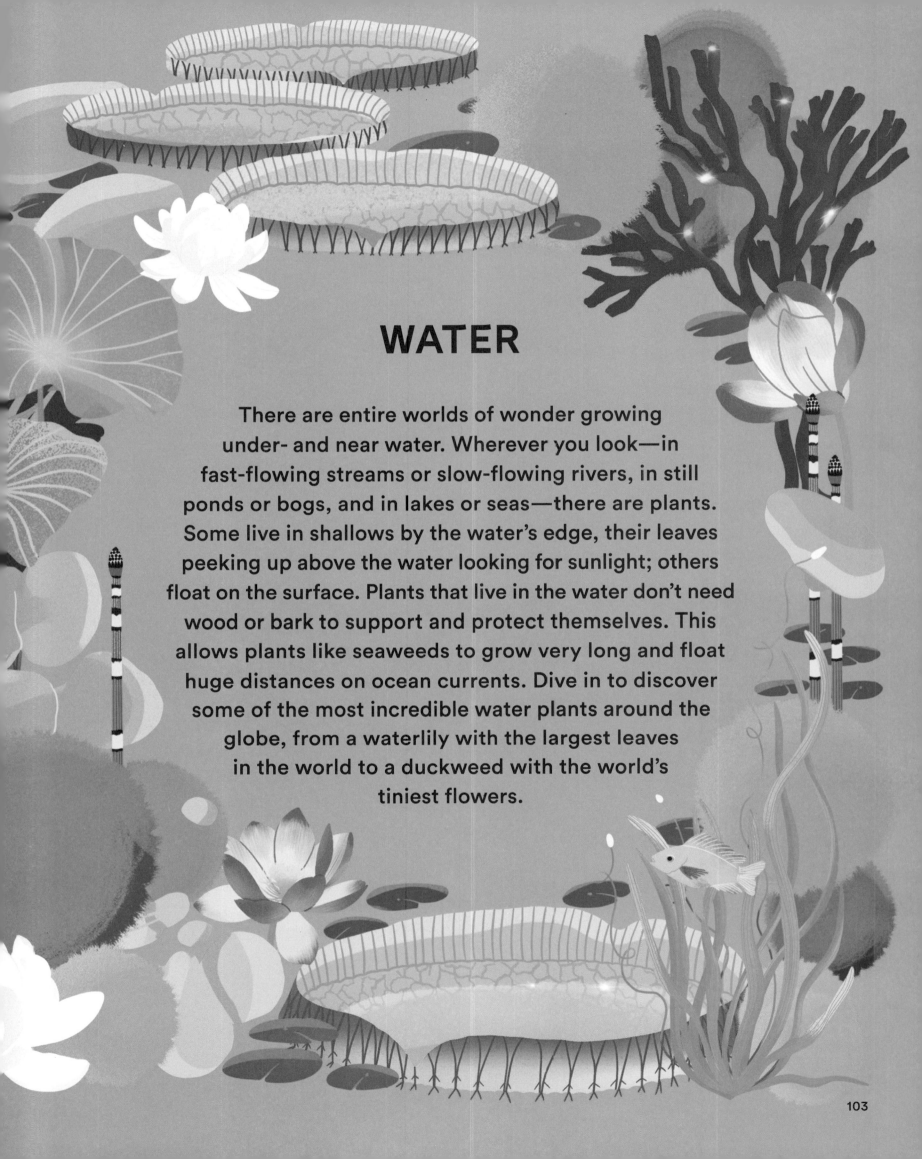

WATER

There are entire worlds of wonder growing under- and near water. Wherever you look—in fast-flowing streams or slow-flowing rivers, in still ponds or bogs, and in lakes or seas—there are plants. Some live in shallows by the water's edge, their leaves peeking up above the water looking for sunlight; others float on the surface. Plants that live in the water don't need wood or bark to support and protect themselves. This allows plants like seaweeds to grow very long and float huge distances on ocean currents. Dive in to discover some of the most incredible water plants around the globe, from a waterlily with the largest leaves in the world to a duckweed with the world's tiniest flowers.

Fast-Flowing Rivers

The Caño Cristales river in the Colombian tropical rain forest is 621 miles long. It is very fast flowing in the rainy season with lots of rapids. Torrents of water rush over rocks and over boulders, so plants living there have to cling on tight. Most of the year the river is a dark-green underwater forest of red macarenia plants. In the dry season, when the water is shallow and the sunlight is strong, these plants change color, turning the river so vibrant, it gets called the Rainbow River, the River of Five Colors, and the Liquid Rainbow.

Red Macarenia
Macarenia clavigera

Much like a deciduous tree's leaves change from green to red in fall, this plant turns blue, green, brown, black, red, yellow, and even pink throughout the year.

To handle the fast current, their flexible stems and branches move with the flow of the water.

Thin feathery stems called filaments form at the end of their branches.

These filaments look like leaves but behave like roots, taking in the minerals and nutrients—phosphorous and iron—dissolved in the water as it flows over the rocks.

This plant doesn't bury its roots in the ground. Instead, the stems attach themselves to the riverbed rocks like superglue. The rock will break before these roots lose their grip!

Streams

Like rivers, streams can provide habitats for plants and animals that depend on running water. Eelweed can be found in many different countries, making it one of the most widespread aquatic plants on Earth. It is native to warm climates in southern Europe, northern Africa, the Middle East, and Asia. It forms lush green underwater meadows, creating shelter for fish. People grow it in their fish tanks, as tropical fish love it, but this causes problems when it escapes into the wild. It is long-lived, fast-growing, and it takes over from the native species.

Eelweed
Vallisneria spiralis

This extraordinary plant has found a clever way to spread its pollen and seeds from its underwater home.

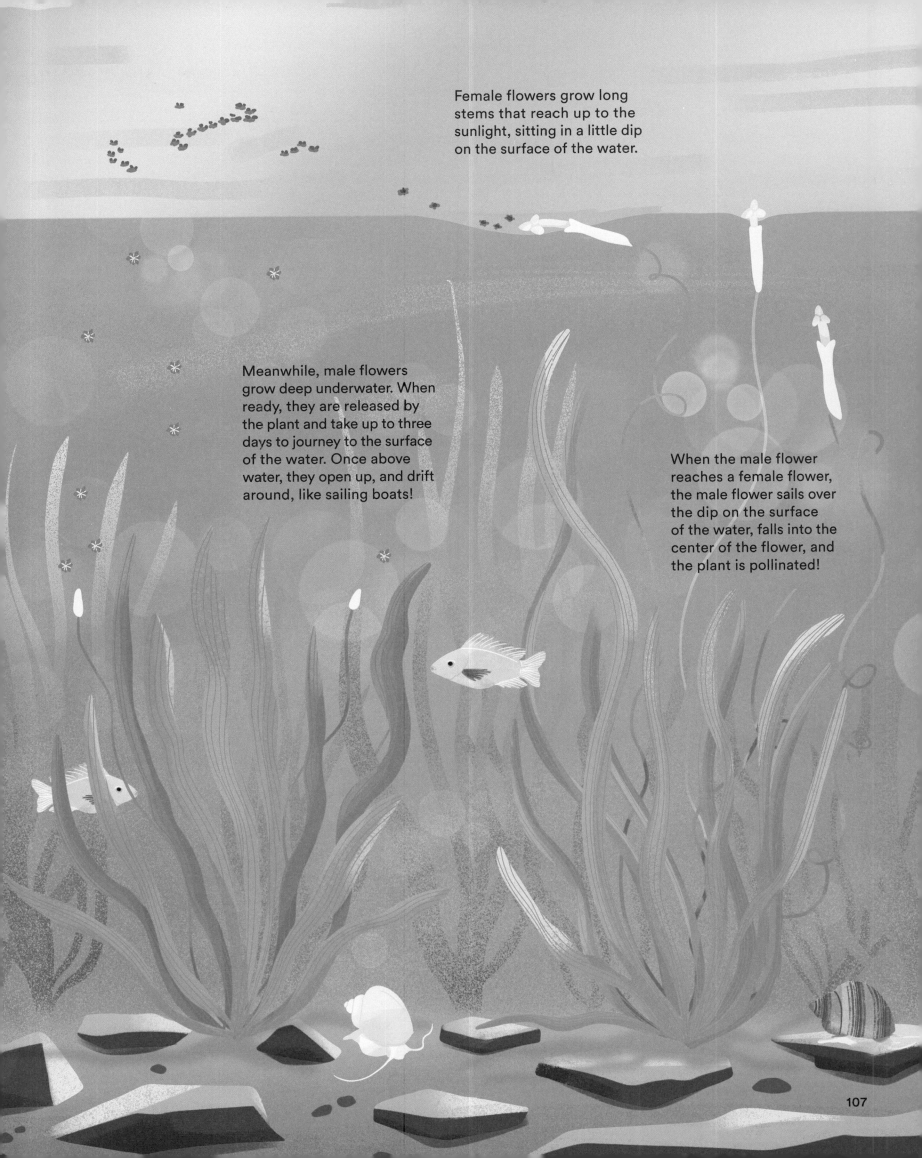

Female flowers grow long stems that reach up to the sunlight, sitting in a little dip on the surface of the water.

Meanwhile, male flowers grow deep underwater. When ready, they are released by the plant and take up to three days to journey to the surface of the water. Once above water, they open up, and drift around, like sailing boats!

When the male flower reaches a female flower, the male flower sails over the dip on the surface of the water, falls into the center of the flower, and the plant is pollinated!

Cold-water Lakes

Lakes are an important habitat for mammals, fish, crustaceans, water birds, and plants. Many lakes appeared after glaciers moved across the Earth during the last Ice Age, leaving behind giant hollows that filled with rain and **groundwater**. Others, like Lake Akan in northern Japan, were formed in the craters of extinct volcanoes. In some of these cold water lakes—in Japan, Iceland, and parts of Northern Europe—a special kind of algae grows.

Marimo
Aegagropila linnaei

These perfectly round velvety balls of algae huddle together on the lake bed. Scientists believe there could be up to 600 million marimo in Lake Akan alone!

In winter, flattened lumps of this algae are also found along the lakeshores. When the ice melts in spring, the algae washes into the water and its shape starts to change.

Marimo algae balls are normally found where the water is 6.5–8 ft deep.

The wind makes currents in the water that gently spin the marimo into balls.

As they slowly spin, each part gets time in the sunlight, allowing it to keep growing.

Sunlight helps the plant make oxygen. This oxygen is often trapped in the strands of algae, making some of the balls float to the surface during the day and sink to the bottom of the lake at night.

Marimo balls are often small—no bigger than a walnut, but some are as big as basketballs. They can take up to 100 years to grow this size!

Marimo are popular aquarium plants, as they purify the water. They do this by naturally filtering out poisonous chemicals in the water.

In Japan, marimo have been designated a "Special Natural Monument." There are marimo lucky charms, toys, and even cartoons!

Tropical Wetlands

Wetlands are found throughout the tropics. Some are wet all year-round, but many only flood in the rainy season, covering savanna grasslands or rain forests many feet deep in water. One wetland, called the *Pantanal*, stretches across Brazil, Paraguay, and Bolivia. It covers an area three times the size of Switzerland. Lots of extraordinary plants live in wetlands, but one incredible waterlily is giant among them all. A prized plant in botanic gardens, it is famous for having the largest leaves of any plant in the world, with football-sized flowers.

Giant Waterlily
Victoria boliviana

The leaves of this recently discovered waterlily can grow up to 20 in a day to over 10 ft across. One plant alone can have 40 leaves, blocking out sunlight for other lake plants.

The giant waterlily's pineapple-scented white flowers bloom in big groups in the evening, attracting flying scarab beetles not only with their fruity fragrance but with a heated, cozy shelter!

The beetles crawl down into the flower, where it is about 50°F warmer than outside.

Spines on the undersides of their leaves stop them from being eaten, and push other plants out of the way.

Pollen from the last flower the beetles visited rubs off and pollinates the plant.

Then the pollinated part of the flower cools down and another part of the flower heats up, drawing the beetle to the new, cozier place where they can pick up more pollen.

The leaf is covered in tiny holes and has a slightly raised center and a v-shaped notch in the side, all to help rainwater drain quickly so it doesn't sink.

After the pollen-covered beetle has crawled out and flown away, the flower turns pink and dies, with seeds forming in its place.

Temperate Shorelines

Where the land meets the sea, the shoreline constantly changes as the tide goes in and out. *Chondrus crispus*, also called carrageen or Irish moss, is one of a group called the red seaweeds. The other two main groups are green and brown. Irish moss is found in shallow water, rock pools, and estuaries on temperate shorelines around Britain, Scandinavia, and parts of North America and the Pacific. Fish and small crustaceans hide among the fronds.

Irish Moss
Chondrus crispus

Although this small seaweed is called a red seaweed, it can be dark purple or purplish brown. Sometimes the frond tips are bright blue. It looks like giant parsley, especially when it turns green in bright sunlight.

Irish moss sheds its skin to clean off microscopic creatures and algae that attach themselves to the fonds. This helps it to photosynthesize properly.

Young sea urchins, mussels, crabs, and starfish hide among big colonies.

Seaweeds attach themselves to the seabed or rocks with holdfasts, which are rootlike structures that anchor plants to one place. Unlike roots, they are not used for absorbing food.

Carrageenan, harvested from Irish moss, has many important uses for humans.

Used to thicken cottage cheese, chocolate, ice cream, and jelly . . .

. . .and also in cosmetic creams.

It is used by brewers to remove cloudiness and make beer clear and bright.

It can be used in vegan food instead of animal gelatin.

It is used as a food supplement for horses, sheep, and cows.

What a useful seaweed!

Still Water

Water in ditches and small ponds hardly moves at all. Any currents are created by the wind rather than tides. Some plants thrive in these conditions, like this duckweed, which floats around on ponds, lakes, and ditches in India and Bangladesh. Shaped like a little plate balanced on a stick, it is the smallest flowering plant in the world. It is one of thirty-eight types of plant called duckweed because they move from place to place on the feet of water birds, especially those with webbed feet. These small plants cover big areas. Look out for other kinds of duckweeds in ponds, canals, and lakes near home.

Duckweed
Wolffia microscopica

When you are very small, you need to produce lots of children, quickly, to make sure no one steals your space. This plant shows us how it is done.

Wolffia is a distant cousin of the titan arum. The smallest and largest flowers in the world are related. Isn't that extraordinary?

114

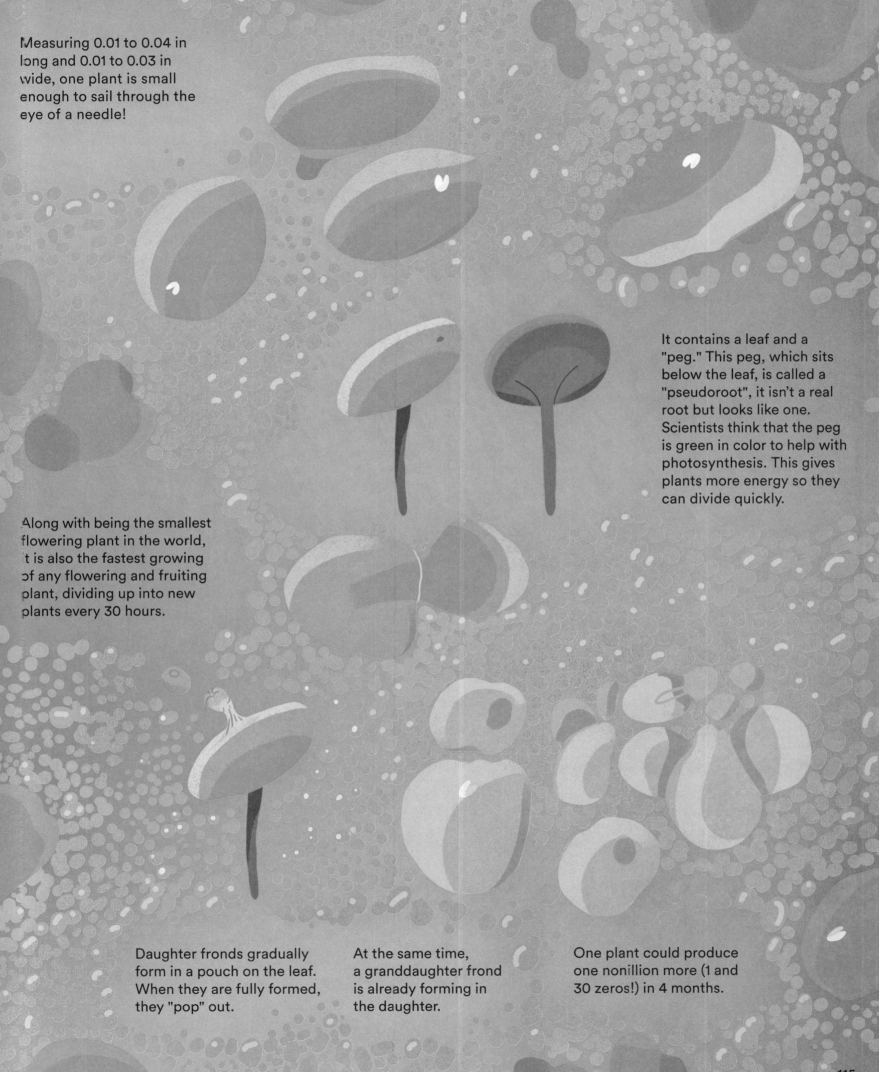

Measuring 0.01 to 0.04 in long and 0.01 to 0.03 in wide, one plant is small enough to sail through the eye of a needle!

It contains a leaf and a "peg." This peg, which sits below the leaf, is called a "pseudoroot", it isn't a real root but looks like one. Scientists think that the peg is green in color to help with photosynthesis. This gives plants more energy so they can divide quickly.

Along with being the smallest flowering plant in the world, it is also the fastest growing of any flowering and fruiting plant, dividing up into new plants every 30 hours.

Daughter fronds gradually form in a pouch on the leaf. When they are fully formed, they "pop" out.

At the same time, a granddaughter frond is already forming in the daughter.

One plant could produce one nonillion more (1 and 30 zeros!) in 4 months.

Growing Water Plants at Home

When caring for these water plants, remember that in their natural habitat, they are surrounded by water all year-round.

Rough Horsetail
Equisetum hyemale

This plant, with stems like a bamboo, is an **early land plant** from eons ago. It comes from cooler temperate areas so will grow well in cool climates. Grow it around the edge of a pond or in a pot of soaking wet multipurpose or soil-based compost. There can be up to 4 in of water over the compost. Plant it so the rising or setting sun shines through the evergreen stems. When it does, they glow bright green. They also grow in shade, spreading slowly by underground stems. Cut off any frost-damaged stems in spring when the new shoots start growing.

Sacred Lotus
Nelumbo nucifera

You will see this beautiful tropical waterlily in lakes and ponds throughout the tropics and warmer regions of the world. In warmer climates, grow them in full sun in a pool, in a container in soil-based compost. As the plants grow, gradually lower the containers. The soil in the container should have at least 2–4 in of water above it. In cool areas, gradually reduce the water level in early fall and store the container over winter in a frost-free place, keeping the compost just moist. Dwarf varieties are better for small gardens. They need at least 75°F for at least 3 months in summer to do well.

Nymphaea

Nymphaea "Pygmaea Helvola"

Grow this small deciduous waterlily in still water, on the edge of a pond or large bowl. The plant should be 5.5–8 in deep. Plant in baskets in aquatic plant compost with the point it grows from just below the soil surface. Cover the compost with pea shingle. Raise the basket so the leaves are covered by 3–4 in of water. An empty upturned planting basket will do. As the stems grow, gradually lower the plants until they are 8 in below the surface. Feed during the **growing season** with an aquatic plant fertilizer. Cut off yellowing leaves and dead blooms. The plant goes dormant in winter.

Water Hawthorn

Aponogeton distachyos

You will often see this white-flowered plant growing in garden ponds in temperate climates, as these plants like cold water. The leaves lie flat on the water. Stems and flowers appear in spring, go dormant in summer if the water gets too warm, then reappear in fall. Plant it up to 24 in deep, in baskets of aquatic plant compost, in sun or part shade. They flower for longer in cooler temperatures. They can also grow in slowly moving water.

Growing Plants at Home

Every plant that grows helps to produce the oxygen we breathe and absorbs the carbon dioxide we produce. The more we grow, the more we help the planet. You can grow plants in gardens and courtyards, on balconies and windowsills, and in rooms in your house. All they need is light, moisture, food, and soil or compost. Treat them like your pets and take care of them. Growing plants is super fun! Here are some tips to get you started.

Let's sow some seeds!

You will need

❋ **Container**

No need to buy something new—an egg carton, butter tub, or even an ice-cream tub will do! Ask an adult to help you make some holes in the bottom of a container for drainage. If you buy new pots, try to find sustainable pots made of recycled plastic or bamboo fiber.

❋ **Compost**

Use peat-free compost from a store.

❋ **Seeds**

When sowing seeds, leave a gap between the top of the compost and the rim of the container. This stops the water from going over the sides when you are watering. Cress, arugula, sunflowers, radishes, and peas for shoots are great seeds to start with.

❋ **Labels**

Make labels from old yogurt containers or lollipop sticks and write down the type of plant and date planted. You can give it a name, too!

Fill the container with compost not quite to the top.

Gently pat down the compost.

Sprinkle with seeds.

Cover the seeds lightly with compost.

Water.

Put them on a sunny windowsill. Water every few days.

Want to plant a bulb instead? Plant them in the ground in soil or in a pot of compost at 2.5 times the depth of the bulb.

Let's grow plants . . . from other plants!

You will need

- A pair of sharp scissors
- Shoot tip from a plant
- A glass, jar, or clear pot
- Tap water
- A container or plant pot
- Compost

Growing plants from other plants is called **propagating**.

Lots of houseplants will root this way. You could try the Swiss cheese plant, lavender, and mountain avens.

Cut a young stem just below a leaf joint, at least 3 in away from the shoot tip.

This is called a cutting. Remove the lower leaves. Any leaves in water will rot.

Put the cuttings in water in a warm place away from bright sunshine.

When roots form and have grown to ½ to ¾ in long, it is ready to plant.

Fill a container with compost. Make a hole in the compost with your finger.

Place the roots carefully in the compost and gently pack the compost around them.

Trickle the water slowly and gently over the compost and allow it to drain.

Put the pot in a bright place away from scorching sunshine.

Once your new plant starts growing, move it to the kind of growing conditions it likes.

Caring for Plants at Home

Check your plants every day to see if they need feeding or watering. You need to see if there are any problems. Plants are like people. A healthy plant is a happy plant.

WATERING

Give plants too much water and they may drown. Give them too little and they can die of thirst.

If you are not sure if your plant needs watering, push your finger into the compost and pull it out. If there is compost sticking to your finger, your plant does not need watering. If there isn't, then your plant needs a drink. Or lift up the container and feel how heavy it is when it has just been watered. The pot will be much lighter when the plant needs watering.

Give your plant a good soaking rather than a little sprinkle. Water houseplants on a dish rack, in the shower pan or bathtub. Leave the pot for half an hour to drain.

Use rainwater for your plants if you can; otherwise, use tap water. Houseplants need warm water. Water plants when they are growing with enough to stop them from dying in winter.

CARING FOR YOUR PLANT

Check your plants every day for pests like slugs and insects. Your local garden center can help you with controlling them in an environmentally friendly way.

You can also buy plant food from garden centers to help your plants grow.

WHERE TO PUT YOUR PLANT

In this book you have learned all about six climatic zones where plants grow. Think about where your plants grow in the wild, then try to copy those conditions. Plants must have enough water and nutrients, light to photosynthesize, and the right temperature for them to grow.

REPOTTING

Plants need repotting every two or three years. Do this in spring as they start growing. Take the whole plant carefully out of the pot so you can see the roots. When the container is almost full of roots, put it into a pot that is ½ an inch to ¾ of an inch wider, using the same kind of compost.

Where to See Plants

Plants are all around you—at school, in local parks, garden centers, and grown in your home. You can see many more incredible plants in hundreds of botanical gardens all over the world.

El Jardín Botánico de Buenos Aires
Argentina

Royal Botanic Garden
Sydney, Australia

Andromeda Botanic Gardens
Bathsheba, Barbados

Jardim Botânico do Rio de Janeiro
Brazil

Montreal Botanical Garden
Canada

Arctic-Alpine Botanic Garden
Tromsø, Norway

Jardin des Plantes
Paris, France

Bogor Botanical Gardens
Indonesia

La Mortola
Ventimiglia, Italy

Kinkakuji Gardens
Kyoto, Japan

Jardin Majorelle
Marrakech, Morocco

Auckland Botanic Gardens
New Zealand

Singapore Botanic Gardens
Singapore

Kirstenbosch National Botanical Garden
Cape Town, South Africa

Royal Botanic Gardens, Kew
London, United Kingdom

Desert Botanical Garden
Phoenix, Arizona

A HOME FOR EVERY PLANT

From the freezing polar regions to hot humid rain forests, from underwater homes to dry scorching deserts, we have discovered many incredible plants all over the world.

Plants make their homes almost everywhere. They also make their habitat a wonderful home for other living things, whether it's their branches providing a playground for monkeys to swing through, nectar for insects to feed on, or twigs for birds to build their nests from.

But plants are not just important for wildlife. We make our habitat from plants too! We use timber from trees to build houses that we fill with wooden furniture. Plants are used to make medicines to keep us healthy. They provide food, and even our clothes can be made from plants such as cotton and hemp. At school we play games on grass, write with wooden pencils, and use erasers made from tree sap. Plants aren't just useful; they turn our homes, gardens, and neighborhoods into a happy place to live with their beautiful leaves, flowers, and fruit.

Most important, without plants, life on land and in the air would not exist. Plants convert the environment-damaging carbon dioxide we make into the oxygen we breathe. We all depend on plants; without them, nothing would survive.

Wherever they are found, plants are so much more than something to see. Plants and wildlife have a symbiotic relationship—plants depend on us to survive too. They need looking after, with care and attention. Together we can make sure there is a home for every plant.

Glossary

Annuals—Plants that germinate, grow, flower, and produce seeds in one year.

Biodiversity—All of the different kinds of living things found in a particular habitat, including animals, plants, fungi, and insects.

Bulb—Some plants grow from a special stem with overlapping leaves, called a bulb. Tulips and daffodils grow from bulbs.

Bromeliad—A family of tropical plants found mainly in North, Central, and South America. Pineapples are a type of bromeliad.

Climate—The kind of weather in a particular place that happens over a long period of time.

Deciduous—A plant that sheds its leaves all at once. It happens in fall in cold climates and in the dry season in hotter climates.

Dormant—When a plant doesn't grow and rests for a period of time, instead.

Early land plant—The first plants to appear on land, such as mosses and liverworts. They reproduced from spores instead of seeds.

Ecosystem—The relationship between all of the living things in an area and the environment they live in.

Endangered—Plant or animal species that may die out because there are very few of them left in the wild or grown in gardens.

Environment—The surroundings where a plant, human, or animal lives, including the weather.

Epiphyte—A plant that lives on another plant but doesn't take nutrients from it. Such as a bromeliad perched on a tree branch.

Evergreen—A plant that keeps its leaves all year-round.

Free-draining soil—Soil that doesn't hold water, so it dries out quickly.

Germinate—When a seed produces roots and a shoot and starts to grow.

Groundwater—Water from melting ice, snow, or rain can't drain through solid rock, so it flows out through the ground into lakes and rivers. Soil where there is groundwater is often very wet.

Growing season—The months of the year when a plant grows. In temperate climates it is from spring to fall, then plants go dormant.

Habitat—The natural home of a plant or animal, such as a forest or a desert. Plants grow in all habitats.

Herbaceous—A plant producing leaves and soft stems that die down to the ground in winter and are replaced by new growth in spring.

Humidity—The amount of water in the air. Air in the rain forest has high humidity, as it is very wet. Air in the desert has low humidity, as it is very dry.

Microclimate—A small area where the climate is different from the larger surrounding area. It can be just a few square feet and sometimes even smaller.

Nutrients—The different kinds of food a plant needs to keep it alive and that helps them produce roots, stems, leaves, flowers, and fruit.

Parasitic—A plant that steals food from another plant, such as the Western Australian Christmas tree and the western underground orchid.

Perennial—Plants that live for more than two years and usually flower each year.

Photosynthesis—When green plants use sunlight, water, and carbon dioxide to create oxygen and make energy so they can grow.

Pollinate—The movement of pollen from one plant to another. This produces seeds.

Propagation—To create a new plant from part of another, such as seeds or cuttings.

Resin—A very sticky sap produced by some plants.

Saponins—When the woody stems, roots, and leaves of the plants that contain these chemicals are rubbed or swished around in water, they make bubbles. They are a natural source of soap.

Sedge—A plant that is related to grasses and rushes. Many grow in extreme habitats where it is very cold, wet, or dry.

Sediment—Particles of material that are small enough to move around in water. When the water doesn't flow fast enough to carry them along, they sink and settle.

Species—When they breed, the offspring look like their parents and each other. All of the different kinds of lithops are related species.

Taproot—A big main root that stores food and water. Carrots and parsnips are taproots. Welwitschia has a taproot.

Vegetation—All of the plants in a habitat.

Weather—The state of the atmosphere each day: hot, cold, sunny, snowy, rainy.

Index

Acknowledgments

Massive thanks to everyone at Phaidon, particularly Victoria Clarke, for her kindness and taking a chance; Publisher Maya Gartner for her boundless enthusiasm; and Project Editor Alice-May Bermingham for her endless patience, understanding, and guidance. Also, thanks go to illustrator Lucila Perini, who ensured that each picture was worth more than a thousand words; designer Ana Teodoro; production controller Rebecca Price, and Robin Pridy, Kirsten Etheridge, Kaitlin Severini, and the rest of the Phaidon team.

When the eminent botanist Prof. Kingsley Dixon of Curtin University, Western Australia, generously offered to be the botanical checker, I was stunned (and will ever remain so!). Thanks also to the following for so generously sharing your knowledge and ideas: Robert Vernon, Debs Goodenough, Mark Paterson, Ian Thwaites, Don Billington, Blaise Cooke, Sophie Walwin, Ian and Lorie Mastemaker, Chloe Wells, Cherry Carmen, Dr. Jo Elworthy, Dr. Wawan Sujarwo, Dr. Dean Nicholl, Dr. Kate L. Delaporte, Dr. Mike Maunder, Dr. Gwilym Lewis, and Dr. Mark Hershcovitz. From the American Fern Society: Dr. Jordan Metzgar, Dr. Tom Ranker, Dr. Michael Windham, Dr. Amanda Grusz, Dr. Carl Rothfels, and David Schwartz. European Palm Society members Martin Gibbons, Tony King, and John Prescott.

Dr. Corneille Ewango, an inspiration for conservation in action.

Dr. Peter Gibbs, who gave generously of his time and expertise to ensure that the meteorology was correct as our climate changes and offered so much encouragement.

Educationalists Phil Mercer, Suzette Thompson, Juliet Paterson, and Lara Honnor offered ideas and suggested just what 7–11-year-olds would be looking for. Laura Ponsonby for being truly inspirational early in my career.

When reliable sources were needed, Tony Hall and Emma Crawforth recommended alpine expert Matthew Jeffrey, who was so generous with his help and knowledge, as was David Cooke. Thanks also to my dear pal Roy Lancaster, for sharing his passion for wild plants.

Henry Biggs made an introduction to aquatics expert Ollie Lenthall and brewer Will Phoenix; Chloe Biggs was a brilliantly efficient picture researcher at a critical moment. Thanks also to Gill and Jessica Biggs for their support, and to Dan Cockahhh!

Finally, big thanks Jemima Rathbone for her carefully chosen words and enthusiasm at critical moments.

To anyone I inadvertently omitted, my apologies and grateful thanks.

A huge thank-you to you all.

About the Author

Matthew Biggs is a graduate of the Royal Botanic Gardens, Kew, a well-known British gardener, broadcaster, and author of fifteen gardening and plant-related books. He is a panel member on BBC Radio 4's *Gardeners' Question Time*.

About the Illustrator

Illustrator Lucila Perini is based in Buenos Aires, Argentina. Her illustrations can be found in leading publications, advertising campaigns and digital media worldwide, including the *Los Angeles Times*, the *Washington Post*, the *Boston Globe*, Airbnb, Citroën, and more.